# The Man Who Sang Blockbuster

Brian Manly

Brian Manly 2009

*First Published by*

## Somehitwonder**S**

51 e Station Rd
Hendon
London
NW4 4 PN
www.somehitwonders.co.uk
Copyright © **Brian Manly**

**ISBN**
978-0-9562249-0-3

Printed in the UK by
Dolman Scott Ltd
www.dolmanscott.com

**Dedicated** to Sean Body of Helter Skelter publishing.
He believed in my book and in all the stories that came from the "little guys" out there. He set me right on how to write it and then sadly passed away. Here is our book Sean, much the way you wanted it, I'll always appreciate your interest and encouragement.

*****

**I would** like to express my eternal gratitude to the following without whom there would be no Man Who Sang Blockbuster: Dick Barnatt (kind permission to use photos), Sean Body, Norman Dival & Maureen O,Grady ( Tony Barrow agency ), Cos Cimino (Sweet Fan Club), Steven Barrat (Art work), Adrian Daulton (design), Simon Forster (cover photo), and especially Frank Torpey (The Sweet's first Guitarist).
My special thanks go to Steve Preist, who answered every email and gave me permission to use his own biography as a research tool.

*****

**To Nicola Connolly**, I saw your email expressing interest in the project and I also understand that you felt un-able to participate. For you, your sister Michelle and for BC Junior, here is my Biography of Brian Connolly, the man you call dad.

# Note from the Author

**I have** written this book about Sweet primarily to tell the story of Brian Connolly. It was after all he and Mick Tucker who formed the Sweet some forty years ago.

To the general public The Sweet was; Andy Scott, Mick Tucker, Steve Priest and Brian Connolly. They sold tens of millions of records during the 1970s and were the forerunners to Queen.

There have been many schisms, arguments and declarations of war from within the ranks of the band, some for obvious reasons, some because of musical differences and more still that seem to be steeped in jealousy and egotism.

For many years now The Sweet has existed purely as the realm of Andy Scott. Catering for the remaining fans, those who prefer Sweet's heavy metal songbook, Andy earns a grand living in Germany and Scandinavia.

Until recently Steve Priest had not played as a member of Sweet for over a quarter of a century, preferring life in Los Angeles to his native London he has only a casual interest in the music business today.

Sweet's handsome drummer Mick Tucker died in 2002 following a long and brave battle with leukaemia.

What then of Brian Connolly, Sweet's founding member and troubled Star vocalist? His sorry tale has been told many times in Sunday tabloid papers, each time bringing more inconsistencies and in some cases pure fabrication. There were times when he seemed to encourage the Tabloids in their ill researched pieces about his wretched circumstances, ill health, bankruptcy and fall from grace but a drowning man will grab anything that keeps him afloat.

Time and time again while researching this book I have encountered articles about Brian Connolly that simply re hash the same well trodden path of scant biography and cliché. The sentence "attempted a solo career and failed" will not be written again within these pages, Andy, Steve and Mick all failed to "exist" in the eyes of the general public after Sweet ended. Likewise Brian had no hits as a solo artist and managed to record barely an album full of songs but there is a story to tell. Similarly the works that he did manage to record deserve constructive reviews from an informed view point.

In our youth we all have idols from the popular culture around us, my idol was Brian Connolly. As a young lad I would watch him slapping his thigh while performing on Top Of The pops, golden hair blow waved to perfection, his face made up with stars that glittered. I adored him, wanted to be him, I considered him perfection personified. Imagine if you can, a ten year old Gay lad harbouring clandestine feelings for the rugby players he saw on telly, in secret I longed to be as flamboyantly gorgeous on the out side as I felt on the inside! Then one Thursday night my world changed forever. A siren blasted out into twenty million homes across England and ours was one of them.

During a recent visit to Cos Cimino, editor of the Sweet Fanzine, I couldn't resist watching some videos he eagerly pulled off the shelf for me to see. We sat in silence until one particular clip totally captured the luminescent magic of Brian Connolly. Cos is a family man, straight as they come, yet he agreed instantly with my observation that Connolly was "utterly beautiful" In 1973 no one looked or sounded like Brian Connolly, an awful lot of people wished they did, many for commercial reasons. Me? I at last knew that another human being existed who matched my own vision of Brian Manly. We merged, secretly and quietly in my mind, only my hair gave it away as it slowly inched its way down my shoulders. As it turned out, Brian Connolly was only an act, or at least the make up and glitter was. As an icon he is not terribly well remembered today but in his moment he experienced fame bordering on superstardom. For those too young to have been there during Connolly's Glam Rock peak I would offer the vision of Deborah Harry in the Heart of glass video. Brian has few videos as such for MTV to show, he and Sweet flew around the world on a daily basis making live TV appearances. On occasion a producer would film him perfectly, as if in a pop video, when this happened his presence was awesome. When a blonde bombshell explodes the impact is inescapable.

Some years later in 1983 I met him and he broke my heart, stumbling around in a nightclub, saying inappropriate things to a young fan and finally being asked to leave. So drunk was he that he mistook my feelings for him as an idol and offered to "give me one". I was young, blonde and rather pretty so perhaps he mistook me for a girl, most likely he simply didn't know what he was doing. I was left in tears while; he was carried out by his arms and legs, watched by his poor wife Marilyn. Within months he would suffer the infamous dozen heart attacks that would destroy his health forever.

It would seem our idols fulfil a need in us, especially when we are young. They entrap us with their music, art or simple good looks but what they often fail to realise is that the effect is for life. No matter what they may do to send us packing, even death does not break the bond of the fan and the star.

A while after the nightclub incident I met Brian again at a record store in central London. He and two of the band were signing copies of their Greatest hits LP. Out of all those hundreds of people Brian recognised me; even in that dreadful state a year earlier he had a memory of me! It was a memorable night because of the drama caused but not unusual in his world at that time.

He looked at me, frowned and said "Have I met you before, somewhere before?"

"Yes, Baileys in Watford at a Suzi Quattro gig" I said in a very guarded way.

Extending both arms to me he took hold of my hands, squeezed them for a moment and said with total conviction, " I am really sorry about that night, I've changed, I don't do things like that anymore, ok?"

I was delighted; in AA what he did would be called a "Step Nine"
Brian had by this time destroyed his career, his fortune and more sadly his voice. He had almost

died on several occasions following alcohol induced cardiac arrests and looked a decade older than his thirty-nine years. What would he do with himself as the 80s rolled on, how would he ever regain so much lost ground when his force seemed almost spent.

"Sweet star in council flat" proclaimed the tabloids.

That was all more than a quarter of a century ago and I am now much older than he was then. Indeed in writing this book what has struck me is that they were little more than I would consider kids nowadays. Andy, Mick and Steve's careers were all but over by the time they were thirty, their peak coming when they were about twenty five years old.

As far as fans go, I'm not much, ill admit it. I followed Sweet for a dozen years religiously but then my own life and career began in earnest. Having bought a couple of Andy Scott's Sweet's albums I realised that the music he makes is not for me. Though I take my hat off to the man and have a special love for him that has lasted almost forty years, it is Brian whose life really is worth writing a book over.

So, here is my version of the life and work of Brian Connolly, as a fan and a writer I think I owe him this, with thanks for the music, the glamour and more importantly the hope that he gave to a kid on a council estate in 1973.

I also owe him two other things, understanding and honesty.

**BRIAN MANLY**

# Contents

1. Oh little star of Hamilton
2. A tribal thing
3. Sweet little lies
4. Three Perfect Gents & a mini van
5. We're off to see Mr Mellin
6. Slow Motion
7. Lollipop man and the Paper Dolls
8. Get on the line/All you ever get from me
9. Great Scott it's Batman and Robin
10. Torpey: Sweet's Pete Best ?
11. Midnight beneath the stars
12. Alexander Graham who ?
13. Funny how Sweet Co Co can be
14. All the ladies laughing gaily
15. Little Willy...big in America
16. Wig Wam Bam (romantically speaking)
17. Blockbuster
18. Honeysuckle burning in the fires of hell
19. It was like lightning
20. There's something in the air
21. Sweet Fanny Adams
22. Life goes on..But it aint easy after Wainman
23. For God's sake Turn It Down
24. The Fox On The Run Phenomenon
25. Not everybody wants Action
26. Strung Up
27. Aint No Body Gonna Take My Place ?
28. Give Us A Drink We're Sloshed Angels
29. Strictly Off The Record
30. Who's The King Of The Castle
31. Pride Always Comes Before A Fall
32. Batman & Robin Utterly Unstoppable

33. Three Piece Sweet Going Cheap
34. Don't you know a lady
35. Take Away the music
36. Hypnotised
37. April 1983 ... a personal memory
38. A Very Public Upheaval
39. It's all in the name
40. It's Sweet's Hits..another personal memory
41. The Ballroom Mix
42. Stevie Take A Bow
43. Mick Tucker ...A Very Nice Man
44. Andy Scott ...The body of work
45. 2008 ...A personal memory
46. Brian and Alcoholism (the final analysis)
47. Rock Bottom
48. Sweet's Ballroom Blitz Video
49. Monsters of Glam
50. A Def Leopard from heaven
51. Lets Go !!!!!!!!!!!!
52. Stabbed in the back
53. February 9th 1997
54. Chinn Chapman The UK Hit Singles
55. Sweet UK Hit Singles
56. Sweet's German Hit Singles
57. Sweet V Queen (on the German Front)
58. Brian Connolly's entire solo recording output

# Oh Little Star of Hamilton

**Hamilton** Scotland - the maternity wing of the local hospital, a young mother screams in pain as her final push delivers a beautiful child, a boy. The nurse holds the baby toward the exhausted young girl;
"Here pet, you hold him, he's a bonny one"
The girl looks at the infant, her lips curl with emotion then she looks away to the starlit sky beyond the window.
"Just the once" pleads the nurse in no more than a whisper.
The girl turns her head into the pillow, it is her only refuge, she is exhausted from the birth and the months of knowing what she will do when the bastard child is delivered. Sensing the moment has passed the nurse tucks the infant into a wicker basket and carries him away.
As she sobs, silently, alone in a war time maternity hospital the girl knows her decision is for the best, they all said it was, everyone, they cant all be wrong. He was on his way now, on his own journey and she who had brought him into the world only a few moments earlier would not see him again.
That's what she thought, quite rightly for who could have known that the boy in the basket, sleeping quietly would for a while be one of the most visible people on the planet. She would see him

again, and he would still possess her name but that was not for a long time to come. She drifted off to sleep, looking out at the stars, not knowing that she had just given the world its sweetest star of all.

Nurse McManus placed the basket into its wire frame and stared down at the infant. Her mind was made up; she knew all about the poor Connolly girl, only fifteen years old, she had seen her around the town. She had helped many such little ones into the world, especially since the war had started, mostly she didn't get attached, you cant, not to so many but this wee thing, he was different, if the girl had to give him to someone, then it would be to her.

How it actually happened we will never know but Brian Connolly was adopted by Nurse McManus shortly after world war two.

# A Tribal Thing

**The** association between Brian Connolly and Mick Tucker can be traced back to just prior to their time in the band Wainwrights Gentlemen. Both lived north of London, Mick was a native, born in Harlesden, Brian had moved from Hamilton in Scotland to Harefiled Middlesex at the age of twelve. His first taste of performing came while still in Scotland where he would perform country and western songs as a contestant in local talent competitions. Before long he had become a regular performer at pubs in the village of Harefield too and could be relied upon win a first or second prize. At fourteen he joined a local group called the So and So's, sadly no photographs have survived. Life for young Connolly, or McManus as he was then known was uneventful during the late fifties. Harefield is much the same today as it was fifty years ago, a rather picturesque little town with an attractive village green. Brian loved to stand out from the crowd and would often dress up in order to do so; it seems he had show business running through his veins right from the start.
Not many miles away in Harlesden a lad called Michael Thomas Tucker dreamed of playing in a group as a drummer, little did he and his soon to be friend Brian know that their dreams would come true big time. Just around the corner from Tucker in Kilburn lived a lovable rogue by the name of Frank.

He and Mick became friends toward the end of 1962 when Mick began his studies at the Willesden School of Technology. During 1964, guitarist Frank Torpey was playing in a successful outfit called The Tribe. Signed to RCA records the Tribe released several singles, the most successful of which was called "The Gamagouchi'. Torpey and members of his Tribe toured Europe and found some recognition in France where 'The Gamagouchi' record was especially popular.

Shortly after the French expedition Torpey left the band and while on sabbatical from his musical career was invited by his old friend Mick Tucker to attend a Wainwrights Gentlemen show at an air force base in Hi Wycombe. Mick was by now their regular drummer, Frank had seen Tucker play many times before and indeed they had played together in a band while Mick was at college.

Torpey explains; "We used to meet and just run through some numbers with a guy called John, Shadows songs mainly, Mick and me were only lads really, he didn't even have a full drum kit in those days, I kinda lost touch after a while and then joined The Tribe and didn't see Mick again till we met up and he asked me along to see his band play, they had a new vocalist called Brian"

# Sweet Little Lies

**There** are many versions of the events that lead to Brian's discovery of his adoptive status and no one left alive from the era to confirm or deny any of them. What is clear is that he had no idea that he was not a natural born member of the family that he had lived among for almost eighteen years. He had reached an age where passports and birth certificates would be needed to prove his identity and either he found out from the authorities at this stage or his adoptive parents sat him down and told him. Down the years Brian told several versions of the events. What is clear is that, quite understandably, his world was shattered, along with his identity.

His first reaction was to run away and so he promptly joined the Merchant Navy in 1963. This would have been a grand plan except that he was colour blind and also suffered from a gastric ulcer at the time, just thirteen months into his sea faring career he was discharged on medical grounds. During his time away he refused to talk to any of the McManus clan and having found out the name of his real mother, changed his name by deed pole to Brian, Francis, Connolly. Upon returning from the navy he set about launching his career and bid for stardom, he wasn't entirely sure at first if this would be via singing or acting. Having had no real training in acting and lots of experience singing country songs he wisely opted for life as a singer. While at sea young Brian had learned to drink and smoke with the best of them however the combination played havoc with his ulcer. Health wise Brian had never been particularly robust, at the age of two he had suffered from a bout of infantile meningitis. In 1947 this could easily have turned out to be fatal and though it could never be proven, this nasty brain infection could have set the seeds for a terrible neurological melt down in later life.

Brian only alluded to his early brush with death on a couple of occasions, once to journalist Rosalind Russell in Disc magazine in 1973. Back in 1965 his luck was about to change as the result of an audition with a semi professional white soul band called Wainrights Gentlemen. Following the rift with his adoptive family he was keen to show them that he could make it in the world without them. Though it may have been common enough for families to hide the truth from adopted children during the fifties and sixties, Brian's reaction was far from uncommon. As far as Brian was concerned he had been lied to and betrayed, not just on the adoption issue but on everything, it had all been a lie. Just as Francis Connolly had rejected him at birth, he had now rejected the McManus family. By day he worked in a succession of sales jobs, eventually settling in at Vicmons of Uxbridge. Vicmons sold carpets and Brian was by all accounts rather a good salesman. Musically, although he still loved his old favourites, Nat King Cole, Hank Williams and the Everly brothers he had also developed a taste for more modern acts like the infamous trouser splitting PJ Proby. Proby was to become as famous for his stage antics as his recordings. One of the first people

Brian noticed when he tried out for Wainrights Gentlemen was their flamboyant and good looking drummer Mick. Though never a great musician, from day one Brian worked out that the people who really make it in show business have a strong individual image, if not a whole hearted gimmick. They also tend to have one other "quality"; they are ruthless in their pursuit of success. As far as he was concerned from the moment he had discovered the truth about his roots, Brian had, to some degree become a non entity.

Following the change of name he was determined that Brian Connolly as he was now known would become Brian somebody.

# Three Perfect Gentleman and a Mini Van

**The** name Wainright's Gentlemen has, down the years, become synonymous as a part of the story of Brian Connolly and the Sweet. Purely by association this semi professional band of five players, who never even recorded a song together, has found a place in Rock history.

Playing a soul based repertoire of R&B standards interspersed with Motown favourites the band found regular work on Army and Air force bases in Ruislip and Northolt, just north of London. Occasionally they would find work in London itself at dance halls.

The main players were Ian Gillan (vocals) Mick Tucker (drums) Tony Hall on Saxophone and a shifting set of Guitarists.

When Ian Gillan left the band toward the end of 1966 he created a vacancy promptly filled by, Brian Francis Connolly. Gillan would go on to world fame with Deep Purple but prior to that he would leave a footprint in the Sweet's story by way of the song 'Questions'. Recorded in 1968 as a batch of prospective singles not released on the Fontana label, Questions sounds quite unlike anything Gillan would create again. Despite his reputation as a consummate Heavy Rock merchant, Gillan also sang on the original album recording of the show Jesus Christ Superstar. His biographies quietly omit any mention of his months as a Gentleman along with Tucker, Hall and co, or indeed the pop track he wrote Sweet in 1968.

Unable to earn a living in a semi professional five piece band, the players in Wainrights Gentlemen had to work "day jobs" to keep a roof over their heads. Having finished his studies at Willesden's school of Technology Mick promptly found work as a car mechanic locally not far from his home in Torcross Road Ruislip. Being good with motor vehicles was a positive asset for the young drummer who had acquired a Grey Mini Van.

Brian continued to earn a living during the day working as a salesman at Vicmons Carpets of Uxbridge. He lived nearby in a flat with new girlfriend Marilyn, coincidentally he too now owned a Grey Mini van though his was not as well kept as Mick's and was apt to break down.

During their time in Wainrights Gentlemen Brian and Mick forged a very close friendship and a bond was created that would last for the rest of their lives. After work on evenings when the band was not playing they would enjoy a beer at their favourite local pub, The Swan. Brian showed great vocal promise during his time in Wainrights Gentlemen, his voice was especially suited to the Motown material often covered by the band, one song in particular displayed the distinctive quality of his voice, Reflections, a hit at the time for Diana Ross.

One evening in 1967 Torpey was invited on stage at a gig in Harrow where his guitar skills were quickly recognised, he was offered a job with the band and he readily accepted. For some reason never as yet explained Wainrights Gentlemen was a band more unstable than the san Andreas fault line and it wasn't long before Torpey was fired, followed swiftly by Tucker who it was felt was too flamboyant and loosing interest in the band. Brian had no intentions of becoming the Gentlemen's next victim and so went immediately to see Mick to suggest that they form their own group. Careless in the extreme Wainrights Gentlemen had now lost two of the coming decade's most famous vocalists and one of its most talented drummers! The group were no more within two years and have been written about for the last forty purely because of who left the band rather than who remained.

Now banished from the "Gents" Brian and Mick set the ball rolling immediately, old friend Frank Torpey would provide guitar which left a vacant slot for a base player. They had two main requirements, number one that the applicant should be able to play base guitar and number two that he should be able to sing harmonies with Brian and Mick. Frank was not a part of the new group's vocal sound though he too had the ability to "carry a tune"

Mick knew of such a person, Steven Priest who was at that time in a group called the Army. Shortly before his relatively brief stint with the Army Priest was with a band called The Countdowns. At Mick's suggestion the three lads went to see Priest performing with the Army and immediately made him an offer to join their as yet unnamed musical venture. The Army was a strange group that started as a four piece and collected new members with alarming speed, by the time Steve Priest decided to leave there were nine or ten people crammed onto small college stages. The size of the group was a major consideration for Steve's decision to leave. In his own words "we were never paid very much for our shows and with all those people in the band there was rarely much in the way of wages". Steve lived in Hayes Middlesex just North West of London and about fifteen minutes from where Brian and Mick were living.

The four young musicians gelled very quickly, Priest's voice being an excellent contrast to Connolly's and Tuckers; the blending was perfect. Once again they were playing a set heavily laden with soul music, indeed 'Soul Man' was a Wainrights "cover song" quickly incorporated into the set, another Motown hit sung by the fledgling Sweet was Diana Ross and the Supremes hit You keep me hanging on. During this early period, with his vocal chords in perfect condition Brian really could do such material beautifully.

Things moved rather quickly by all accounts, the four working during the day and spending hours each night rehearsing, often in a garage in Ruislip. Brian was determined not to waste any more time as a semi professional, he was twenty two years of age, perfect for a pop breakthrough. Just ten weeks after the new band was formed Brian had enough confidence to show it to the world or at least some influential people he had gotten to know in the world.

# We're Off to See Mr Mellin

**After** forty years there are few left alive to tell the story of the signing of The Sweet shop's first recording contract. Guitarist frank Torpey recalls that Brian knew a singer by the name of Paul who was employed by Mellin's music co. Roger Mellin was a successful music publisher whose career dates back to the mid 1950s. He had associations with the Phillips recording co, who's off shoot label Fontana would release Sweet's first record. At Brian's suggestion the lads went to visit Paul to see if any doors could be opened. At the time Paul Nicholas had yet to achieve any of the huge success that would be his during the 1970s and 80s. His stage and recording career would include staring roles in Lloyd Webber productions and several disco hits in the mid seventies. During the 80s he enjoyed several years as a sit com star in his series Just good friends.

Back in 1967 he was simply a friend of Brian's and a very useful one as it turned out. Following a meeting with Mr Mellin as he was known the band was introduced to a young drummer and song writer called Phillip Wainman. Wainman was by all accounts keener than keen to produce the group after being blown away by their harmonic skills. During the mid 60s and 70s a good beat and harmonies were essential if a record was to be picked up on radio. Wainman fully understood this and always went for a solid drum track and first rate vocal harmonies.

Despite producing the single 'Slow Motion' beautifully, the credit for production went to Mr Mellin, not young Phillip Wainman. This is a common occurrence in the music business; Mellin also shares a writer's credit for a song recorded as a possible solo single for Brian called "I'm on my way". Its doubtful that "old man Mellin" was actually writing or producing pop records in the 60s, far more likely that he was an executive producer having been the financial backer and publisher of the songs. In his Biography "Ready Steve" Priest claims that the other songs the band were forced to record were written by Mellin's nephew. 'Slow Motion' was written by a man, or perhaps woman called Watkins. Nothing is known of the writer today, indeed Watkins may simply have been a name used for writing purposes.

The name The Sweet is said to have come about because the band rehearsed above a Sweet shop in Harlesden, North London. Legend goes that it was Mick Tucker who picked the name, however Torpey dismisses this and claims that the name came from the 'ether' and was one of two choices, the other name for the band being the cheery sounding "Tears".

Luckily the four plumbed for The Sweet Shop, however when time arrived to sign their first publishing and recording contract it was discovered that another group had taken the name so the decisive Mr Mellin scribbled out the word shop and The Sweet was born. Brian's girlfriend Marilyn was forced to eat humble pie as her faith .in Brian's destined stardom was not always as strong as his, now he had actually gone and made a record.

# Slow Motion

**The** Fontana label had seen the release of many successful singles during the 1960s so there was much hope when The Sweet released Slow Motion in July 1968.
Apart from writing and producing for themselves in later years, the early singles with Fontana and Parlophone are solid evidence to contradict those who claim that Sweet were an invention of songwriters Nicky Chinn and Mike Chapman.
 They were in fact, early pioneers to some degree, the notion of a pop group having existed for only four or five years prior to them forming the Sweet. The Beatles had begun a trend earlier that had set pop music galloping in its development. Mick and Steve in particular liked the music of a new group called Cream. One of Cream's more popular of five top thirty hits, 'Sunshine Of Your Love', would follow 'Slow Motion' in October 68.
 Cream was truly ground breaking in 1967 all but launching the career of the great Eric Clapton. Prior to Cream Clapton had cut his teeth with the Yardbirds.
 'Slow Motion' saw the emergence of a new Brian Connolly, his performance is excellent, as are most other aspects of the recording. A real slice of the swinging sixties, the band provided little more than vocals for the record as was the custom in the days when recording studios were the domain of session

players and pop singles were produced live in one or two takes. As outstanding as it was, 'Slow Motion' did not receive a significant amount of airplay and failed to make the charts. In August 1968 the band recorded two sessions for the BBC at the Piccadilly theatre in London. It had been brief but the members of Sweet had tasted some recognition, if not fame, as with all good things, they wanted more. Sadly Fontana and Mellin's music did not see a future for Brian and his comrades and so in October 1968 their deal ended. They continued to find work in clubs and air force bases till the end of the year when, just like Mellin and Fontana, Torpey decided that there was no future to be found hanging around in Sweet. As he had never sung a note, the bands harmonic structure vocally was unaffected. Shortly before he left the band Frank luckily escaped a run in with the law.

It was on an October evening on the way home from a gig with Sweet. Brian and Steve dropped Frank outside his flat off Kilburn High Road. It was after midnight as Brian and Steve headed north along the Edgware Road when they spotted an irresistible sight. There, neatly piled in crates at the side of the road were hundreds of bottles of milk waiting to be picked up by a milk float. Steve pulled over and the pair helped themselves to a few pints, no sooner had they pulled off the foil tops than a Policeman arrived. It turned out that this was a crime "hot spot" and the dairy had had enough. Brian and Steve were escorted to the local police station and arrested, spending the night in the cells. In the morning they had to appear before the magistrate but were given no time or tools to wash and brush up. Seeing two long haired layabouts before him the Magistrate promptly found Messer's Connolly and Priest guilty as charged and fined them twenty pounds a piece. Neither had any money, Marilyn had to help Brian pay his fine while Steve returned to the court a week later with his hair slicked back and wearing his best suite, fully appreciating the nice young lads difficult financial situation the court agreed to let him pay in instalments. From then on Steve never forgot the impact that his image could have upon people.

# Lollipop Man &
# The Paper Dolls

**After** a month or so adrift without a manager or a lead guitarist the newly formed Sweet were taken under the care of Roger Easterby who was having considerable success with the group Vanity Fair. Mean while Mick had found them another guitarist, a lad named Mick Stewart. The new boy had little time to prepare himself before he was off on the Sweet bandwagon, they were growing in popularity on the gig circuit and Easterby had secured them a recording contract with Air Music on the EMI Parlophone label. First up was probably one of the worst records ever made and definitely the one truly horrible disc to be issued by Sweet. The song was written by the winning team of Hammond and Hazelwood, whose songs were apt to be at the sharp end of the bubble gum market. The song 'Lollipop man' was hated by all in the group, they simply had no choice in what their debut EMI offering would be. 'Lollipop Man' deserves no more time spent on it than it takes to play, just one play!

While the nucleus of Connolly, Tucker and Priest were not enamoured with their second singles offering, their new guitarist Mick Stuart let it be known that he was not happy at all to be associated with such nonsense, however at this point in time and for some years to come Sweet were in the business of 'making it', by hook or by crook. Shortly after the stillbirth of 'Lollipop Man' Easterby got the band a job backing a girl group on tour. The Paper Dolls had recently scored a huge hit with a real cracker of a song 'Something Here In My Heart'. Sweet had to learn that hit and five or six other numbers to accompany the girls on tour. There were a few try out shows in London and then both groups headed for Manchester to complete a three week run at the La Dolce Vita night club. In his book "Ready Steve" Steve Priest describes the tense rehearsals with the three members of the Dolls. He particularly didn't like the lead singer Tyger who treated the Sweet as hired hands and backing musicians, which is exactly what they were. The other girls were called Spider and Copper. By all accounts the work went well once they were in Manchester. In order to qualify for his share of the wages Brian went on stage and mimed with an unplugged electric guitar.

This worked for a while until one night he had had a few to drink and didn't realise that the thing was indeed still plugged in. Tyger and co were singularly unimpressed by the terrible racket he had made throughout their show and insisted that Sweet were fired. While at the club Steve and Brian figured out a way of getting through the shutters of the bar after closing time and during their stay helped themselves to copious amounts booze and cigarettes. This was discovered and didn't help their case when the Dolls kicked up a fuss about Brian's guitar fiasco. Two weeks into the engagement the band were sent packing.

As 1969 progressed the bands work began to slow up, they were still working once or twice a week but many venues had already booked them several times. Brian was now twenty- four ,just past the perfect age for pop stardom, fortunately his blonde hair and clear complexion seemed immune to the nights of heavy boozing he frequently indulged in. Steve was the baby of the band, just twenty years of age, followed closely by Mick Tucker who was a year older. Mick Stewart had not gelled fully with the three "original" members of the Sweet but despite this they were a very happy band. Frank Torpey still kept in contact with Brian from time to time and was confident that he had made the right decision in leaving his pals, after all, a few weeks with the Paper Dolls and another flop were hardly causes for celebration or recrimination.

# Get On The Line &
# All You Ever Get From Me

**In** 1970 things were not happening very fast for Sweet, as the months went by it was clear that no real chemistry existed between Brian, Steve and Mick with newcomer Stewart. Though it may have looked good to be releasing not one but two records, live work was certainly slowing down. A log book of Sweet's live performances for 1970 was kept by their booking agent Robert Stigwood and it shows work evaporating toward the end of the year. Had either of the two singles been successful things would undoubtedly been very different.

The first single of 1970 came at the end of January. 'All You Ever Get From Me' is a great little song, a sort of for runner of things to come, it was written by the team of Cook and Greenaway, a popular song writing duo of the late 60s. Although it may have served an established act well, the single lacked the extra sparkle needed to break a new band into the charts. It's a great sound but is clearly from the sixties. Sweet's contract with Parlophone allowed them at last to play on the b sides in the recording studio. Mick the guitarist was having a little trouble settling in as a band member, he was also far more used to playing session work or filling in for musicians on temporary assignments. He did provide the band with two excellent songs by way of

The Juicer and Mr McGallagher but his days in the band were numbered.

Entirely different to Sweet's first single of 1970, "Get On The Line" is an all out assault on the bubble gum/hippie pop market but again it was a little late to be breaking in a band with such a well used genre.

Brian's voice is smooth and clear on both songs; indeed he is the only member of the band performing on the latter. The backing vocals on 'Get On The Line' are provided by The Ladybirds who sang backing on many TV variety shows of the day. The instruments were played entirely by session men. If ever there was a moment for Brian to go solo it was now, this was, to all intents and purposes a solo record but it was not a good time for male vocalists of his kind, this was the golden age of the "pop group" singers were considered old hat.

'Get On The Line' was released in Mid May and picked up for airplay on one or two stations. It was also released in Holland where it did well but for the fourth time in a row Brian and co suffered the humiliation of a flop single. Although some bands such as Status Quo managed to recover from slight false starts at the end of the 60s going on to reinvent themselves in the 70s, many others could not make the leap from one decade to the next. It is probably just as well that Sweet did not "make it" at the end of the 60s as that is likely to have been their final resting place. It had not gone un noticed by Brian and Mick that their former band mate and fellow victim of the Wainright's axe Ian Gillan was having considerable success with his new group Deep Purple. What made things worse was the fact that Purple were making their own music in the form of a huge single 'Black Night'. This was exactly the kind of music Mick Tucker wanted to be playing. It was a classic case of envy mixed with deference on the part of Tucker and Connolly and it would affect their musical choices and direction in ways both positive and negative. Frank Torpey and Brian Connolly had lost touch with each other by now but Sweet's former guitarist had kept an eye on the EMI singles and he felt assured that his decision to leave was still for the best, another two stiffs were hardly a reason to regret his parting, surely?

# Great Scott!
# It's Batman and Robin

**To** say that Brian was becoming disillusioned by the bands' lack of real success was an understatement, like a woman pushing forty his biological clock was ticking too. As his twenty sixth year approached he realised that time was running out. Publicly he claimed to be in his early twenties, youth is everything to a pop pin up. His looks were holding out but many in the business were loosing faith that he or his group had any future, all except perhaps one very important person.

Phil Wainman had kept a fond eye on Sweet even though he was not involved with them at EMI. Despite still holding Sweet to a contract the company had no further plans to even record the band let alone release any more records. At the end of October 1970 Phil became acquainted with a pair of songwriters by the name of Nicky Chinn and Mike Chapman. Chinn was the son of a wealthy self - made millionaire, dapper, intelligent and charming. Chapman had emigrated from Australia the previous year; was playing in a band called Tangerine peel while working nights as a waiter. On one of those nights he served young Chinn at the Tramp nightclub and the two struck up a conversation about music. Chinn had just had some of his compositions used in the hit movie There's A

Girl In My Soup, this impressed the talented waiter no end.

Before long the two were meeting at Chinn's apartment working on songs together. Chinn had little urgent need to make money but a real need to step out from the shadow of his wealthy, self made father. Chapman needed money. With Chinn and Chapman in Kensington, west London and the slowly sinking Sweet in Harlesden and Hayes they were all practically breathing the same air but it would take a suggestion from Phil Wainman to bring them all together. Documented history makes one thing clear, Chinn and Chapman would make it with or without Brian and Co. Just before they got together with them they had secured a deal via Mickie Most's RAK label to release the song 'Tom Tom Turnaround' with the group New World. This reached Number six in the charts in May 1971 but was in the bag months before anything Sweet had recorded with the pair. Steve Priest quickly named Chinn and Chapman Batman and Robin because, according to him, Chinn would order his partner around in the early days and because he was very well spoken. It is quite true to say that in their first year together all the money for recordings and expenses came from Chinn whose wealth opened many doors and made it all possible.

Brian was seriously considering taking up acting by the latter stages of 1970. A relative in his adoptive family was having some success and had just appeared in the movie Ned Kelly alongside Mick Jagger, his name was Mark McManus.

With breaking point approaching and the end of Sweet on the horizon Chinn and Chapman recorded the backing track to a song that would turn around the fortunes of them all, 'Funny Funny'. Just out of the chart after selling millions worldwide was the Archies bubblegum classic 'Sugar Sugar'. Phil Wainman had already heard some of the pairs demo's and declared that he believed in their potential but not their current batch of songs. "Go away and come up with something like 'Sugar Sugar' he suggested and the fledgling songwriters did just that.

On hearing the song he immediately suggested that Brian, Mick and Steve record the vocals, Chapman had already sung on the demo which was so well produced that its backing track was used on the actual single release. First member of Sweet to hear 'Funny Funny' was Tucker who picked it put of a pile of demos played by Wainman "that's the one" he declared and Wainman nodded in agreement. Soon after Brian and Steve went along too for a listen and within a month they had wriggled out of their EMI contract and recorded their next single 'Funny Funny'.

RCA records were keen to release the song but not before Sweet had found itself a guitarist. In haste they attempted to re recruit Stewart and then Torpey. Wainman was not keen to work with the former and then Torpey declined sensing wrongly that the boys were about to release their fifth and final "stiffy".

In early November Mike Chapman placed an advert in the music press asking for talented Guitarists to attend an open audition in west London. One week later on a chilly Wednesday at 7pm several dozen hopefuls had formed an orderly queue outside the hall in Shepherds bush. It was, according to Steve Priest a very long night, with an ever patient Chapman ushering in the "talent" and then ushering it out again without hurting its feelings. Brian had just gone to a local pub and Steve found a spot to curl up and take a nap when a lad walked in wearing a long over coat and sporting a very long fringe that obscured his features completely. After plugging in his Gibson 335 and failing to get a reaction from the amplifier, the bohemian turned all the controls up to full in an effort to coax the equipment into life. It certainly worked, the story of the ensuing racket has been told many times. The young man apologised and said his name was Andy, Andy Scott. He proceeded to play better than almost anyone else seen that evening. As Brian wasn't there and Chapman had some doubts, Andy was asked to return in forty eight hours for a second ordeal. This time he was only up against three other candidates and being the best singer by far, he was in.

Although 'Funny Funny' was done and dusted there was no b side for the release so Andy suggested he write something. The resultant 'You're Not Wrong For Loving Me' was a beautiful number though once again it was played by session musicians, Sweet provided an excellent vocal contribution. Brian wasn't sure about Scott's suitability, he was only nineteen years old and had rock sensibilities rather than country pop but otherwise at this stage they got along together quite well. 'Your not wrong for loving me' was credited to all four members of the band, ensuring that each would have a quarter of the royalty share from the record.

Nicky Chinn had financed the recording sessions and wanted control over the project so he now became Sweet's manager, despite never having managed a pop group before. Christmas was celebrated with fingers crossed all round and in January RCA records released 'Funny Funny' by the Sweet.

After seven days the record showed up on Radio play lists and then a booking was secured on a kids TV show called Lift off. That seemed to do the trick, 'Funny Funny' then leapt into the chart at an amazing number forty eight in the top fifty. Steve and Brian took themselves along to a branch of Woolworth's in Hayes and just stared at the chart behind the counter in the record department, Steve has stated this as the best moment of his life. 'Funny Funny' proceeded to crawl up the chart, peaking at number thirteen a full ten weeks after its release. Sweet made a short promotional film shot in London's Trafalgar square and naturally Top of The pops made the call to Chinn asking for his band to promote their debut hit. In Germany the record flew up the chart and peaked at a heady number three! After all those years of struggle and failure Brian Connolly was at last Brian some body.

# Torpey: Sweet's Pete Best ?

**From** early in life all Sweet fans have been aware of the name Frank Torpey. Like an uncle who moved to Australia he has existed quietly in another musical hemisphere, a familiar enigma, commanding a strange kind of affection.

Who would be Torpey, the man that not only jumped ship once but then decided not to re embark just as his former band mates were about to set sail on the trip of a lifetime.

Interviewed in 2007 he maintains that he was in many ways blessed not to have become a Glam Rock icon. His tone is cheery and very believable. Though hardly a star he had seen some success while in the Tribe during the mid 60s. He had known Mick Tucker for a decade by the time 'Funny Funny' fumbled its way into the chart.

"The lads came and suggested I re join at the end of 1970 but I'd just had my appendix out and was going on a holiday to re coup, I had a few doubts anyway and then when I saw them next it was on Top Of The Pops. I thought it was great but it looked like a one hit wonder"

Until the close of the decade Frank would have the opportunity to see his former chums on TV in the UK over three hundred times, with radio plays reaching incalculable quantities.

So what did happen to the man who handed the golden ticket to Andrew Scott?

Immediately after his decision not to join Sweet again Frank got himself a short stay assignment with the band Ossibisa and then in early 1971 he worked with an off shoot outfit from them called Assigi.

By all accounts a thoroughly competent and imaginative guitarist, Frank was rarely short of work during Sweet's early years of stardom. Indeed he claims that initially his regular work at London's Top Rank clubs saw him entertaining (as a house band member) bigger crowds than Sweet and earning similar amounts of money.

As 1972 came to a close he joined a band called Crackers who were on the borderline of comedy, in a similar vein to a group of the time called the Barron knights. They were in plenty of demand as a live act throughout 1973. During 1973-74 Frank was working hard as a session player in studios, he also worked on some TV variety shows including a series of the Lulu show in 1974. Trudging down to work at Thames TV in Teddington during the evening shift he must have realised that time was marching on and that he would probably not see a star on his dressing room door. His last try at the big time for his own glory was with a punk band in 1977, The "new" punk outfit were in fact Crackers in another guise. Horrorcomic made some highly credible music in their three years together, so credible that Sanctuary Records re issued the whole of their output on a CD in 2006 titled 'England 77'.

While it is available Horrorcomic's 'England 77' album on Castle Music CMQDC 1263 featuring Frank Torpey on guitar should be viewed as compulsory merchandise to a Sweet fan!

Frank lives in Harrow North London with his pretty wife of thirty years Jan and has recently entered his sixties.

It takes a long stretch of the imagination to believe a man who says he has no regrets after passing by the chance of becoming a Millionaire Rock star but Frank Torpey is very believable. He has had almost forty years to consider his fate and his declaration that "I've had an amazing life, most people aren't pop stars but they are perfectly happy" is somehow quite profound.

# At Midnight Beneath the Stars

**There** was much relief when 'Co Co' took to the charts in June 1971 for it immediately changed the group's status from one hit wonder to international Bubble Gum stars. If all sources are to be believed, 'Co Co', beloved million seller of the early 70s took a little over three hours of a morning to record. At that point the four lads were called in to add their vocals during the afternoon recording session. Also in the chart at the very same time was Chinn and Chapman's third hit, 'Tom Tom Turnaround' sung by New World. New World's record was produced by Mickey Most, Sweet's by Phil Wainman, the common ground being Chinn and Chapman. New world settled at Number six while Sweet very nearly topped the chart with 'Co Co'. It was the start of a trend that would see the group labelled with the slogan, "always the bridesmaids never the brides". Mick Tucker was so relieved to have proven all the critics wrong that he had a special T shirt made that declared Sweet were "two hit wonders". The B side of 'Co Co' was the first indication of Sweet's aspiration to play rock music. 'Done Me Wrong Alright', *was* performed by the group, instruments and all, again they completed the track in a morning. Produced by Phil Wainman, the B side was performed practically live and then edited and corrected with over dubbing and mixing. None of the band members were keen on their singles material to date, they had a shared past with the likes of Ian Gillan and Richie Blackmore, they admired Eric Clapton and Cream yet were now singing a song about 'Co Co' the clown. They were young men whose overview did not stretch to a full appreciation of the music business of the day. Only Brian had really gotten what he wanted at this point in time. He had striven for "stardom" and by the end of June 1971 he was becoming a huge pin up star. How Andy, Mick and Steve must have felt as Sweet's "musicians", who had not even played on the record is easy to imagine. On the day 'Co Co' was recorded Mick Tucker had quite a row with one of the session players as they left the studio, his frustration had become too much to bear. 'Co Co' was a totally planned and contrived pop hit not a "band" type of record at all. If it were made today it would be played solely on computer and synthesizer. In June 1971 Sweet were perfectly capable of playing on such a record but could Chinn and Chapman have trusted them? The solo middle eight section was played on Caribbean steel drum not Andy's guitar and all that was required of Mick Tucker was to keep a steady beat with a Caribbean feel, there was no room for creativity and certainly no room for any of Deep Purple's "jiggery pokery".

'Co Co' hit number two in Britain and topped the charts in Germany swelling Chinn and Chapman's coffers by the day because they were the writers. Brian and Sweet would earn a small amount from their shared b side royalty but the real "new money" would come from getting out on the road. Chinn found them some live work but they had a problem known to many who are catapulted to the top of the chart after only one or two hits. 'Co Co' was huge, truly a massive hit placing Sweet in a headlining position at venues yet 'Co Co' and 'Funny Funny' provided them with only five or six minutes of music to perform, the rest of the show was padded out with Rock n Roll standards and a medley of hits by the Who! Confused though they were at times, the audiences kept coming to Sweet's shows and the band members began to see the fruits of stardom.

Brian bought a Ford Capri and he and Marilyn moved to a modest flat in Hayes North of London. For Brian, being Brian Connolly of the Sweet was becoming a full time job with several interviews and photo shoots per week. He was also very popular with his female fans though they were apt to be little more than ten or eleven years of age. At this point Marilyn saw little threat from Brian's teeny bopper fans and despite being proud of his success, thought the music he was making was "a load of rubbish" she was not alone. The critics were completely dismissive of Sweet as a band; indeed it went beyond dismissive and became vindictive. Publicly all four members declared their happiness with the product, Brian claiming, quite rightly, that it was a very great skill to write good commercial music.

In the decades since Sweet and Deep Purple began their careers much has been written with regard Sweet's credibility when measured against such highly regarded Rock giants. Publicly the players in Sweet have stated many times that they were after becoming a more Purple kind of hue themselves.

Over the years the players in Sweet would internalise much of the scathing critiques that would spray over them in the music press. One manifestation of this resulted in the band taking themselves and their critics too seriously, thus corrupting the natural direction of the Sweet in future years.

From out of nowhere, Chinn and Chapman had bestowed upon Brian, Andy, Mick and Steve the keys to the kingdom, they were now pop stars.

Deep Purple had written their own way into the chart with the song 'Black Knight' but would soon disappear from the singles top 40. In this genre Sweet outperformed them spectacularly from day one.

The consequence of the singles success was that the Sweet's later albums would never be treated with a proper regard in the UK.

As 'Co Co' rested proud at Number two through out the summer of 1971 the die had become cast. The Sweet was a pop group, the beneficiaries of stardom as a direct result of their association with Phil Wainman, Nicky Chinn and Mike Chapman. This was, of course not what they wanted, not what their egos or artistic sensitivities required. Andy and Mick in particular dreamt of a band very different a band that perhaps should have been called Sweet Purple.

# Alexander Graham Who ?

**Had** 'Alexander Graham Bell' been a bigger hit things would have turned out very differently for The Sweet, especially Brian Connolly.
Released in October 1971 the record stalled at a lowly number thirty-three in the UK chart. In Germany it stumbled its way a little higher but following the mighty 'Co Co' the single looked like a comparative flop. It would seem that Chinn and Chapman's attempt to provide Brian with a song containing a sensible narrative, rather than simple multi repeat choruses had failed. Brian had requested a story song like 'Alexander Graham Bell' to give him something "a bit more mature to sing about, not just choruses". At the time he declared the song to be "a fantastic song that should have gone higher". The Sweet was, at this stage little more than the backing musicians in the "Brian Connolly show".

The Sweet's records were produced by Phil Wainman; written by Chinn and Chapman, played by session men and sung primarily by Brian Connolly. 'Alexander Graham Bell' failed to find sufficient takers to hoist it into the top twenty anywhere in the world.

Had Brian's request for a more heartfelt and mature song born a better fruit, the taste of the Sweet would have been forever altered, with perhaps far more strings and trumpets and eventually a band that sounded more like Smokie than Sweet. It is possible that the newly recruited Scott would not have stuck around or indeed that Brian would have become a solo singer with a shifting set of backing musicians.

What actually happened was a very quick musical U turn and a return to what had worked a few months earlier, in times of crisis Chinn and Chapman had no scruples or regard for musical acclaim, when a hit was needed, they delivered.

Despite Sweet stalling somewhat with Mr Graham Bell's rather lame ditty Brian's personal star continued to climb. It soon became obvious that professional help was needed with his and the bands dealings with the press.

Eventually Chinn decided that the bands PR would be handled by Tony Barrow enterprises. Barrow was used to handling all of the big names of the day including Cilla Black, New World and The New Seekers. Brian was a PR person's gift at this time; he was punctual, pleasant and always had something to say for himself. He saw his role clearly as the star of the band, not one if its musicians. He was there to sing it and sell it; the other members were there to play it.

# Funny How Sweet Co Co Can Be

In between trips to Europe to promote their newest hits Brian remained busy recording vocals for the bands first long-playing record.

Sweet's debut album is a charming slice of Bubble Gum pop and easy listening, every inch a product of its day. It was pre dated by an album on the MFP label called Sweet and the Pipkins. This was simply EMI cashing in on the bands huge success by releasing their failed singles and B-sides. Without enough songs by Sweet to actually fill an album they shared the release with a contrived manufactured pop creation. The Pipkins were a duo consisting of Tony Burrows, session singer extraordinaire and songwriter Roger Greenaway. Burrows sang on almost half a dozen hit records during the early 70s the biggest being, 'Love Grows Where My Rosemary Goes' under the guise of Edison Lighthouse. Despite singing on some of the biggest hits of the time, he remained relatively unknown, due to the failure of solo singles in the following years and the fact that his collective hits are credited to different groups. 'My Baby Loves Love' and 'Julie D'ya Love Me' were also sung by him for the band White Plains.

The other half of The Pipkins Roger Greenaway had written many hits with partner Roger Cook, the two Rogers had been responsible for Sweet's single 'All You Ever Get From Me', which ranks among their rare failures.

At this time EMI also re issued 'All You Ever Get From Me' in an attempt to cash in on Sweet's incredible success with 'Co Co'. Neither the single or the, "shared album" made any impact on the charts.

If ever there was a time when Brian Connolly was a solo recording act it was during the making of "Funny How Sweet". The tracks are lightweight pop numbers played by session musicians. The only tracks to appear on the LP that were played by the band were the b-sides of their recent singles.

'Santa Monica Sunshine' and 'Honeysuckle Love' are fine songs that suffer only a little because of weak production and arrangement. Beefed up "just a tad" they would have stood the test of time better than they have. 'Sunny Sleeps Late' is a beautiful song produced remarkably well and sung impeccably by Brian.

'Spotlight' is an interesting track as there, almost hidden in the background of the recording is the first hint of Andy's full potential with regard "the sweet sound". His high vocal harmonies add real dramatic effect to the song. Spotlight had seen the light some weeks earlier as the b-side of 'Alexander Graham Bell'.

Four tracks on the album are credited for arrangement to the Irish music mogul Fiachra Trench. Listening to the tracks in question it is hard to see any particular reason for this except that he was "on duty" that day.

Session player Pip Williams is also credited as arranger on a cover version of the old Diana Ross number 'Reflections', sung beautifully by Brian. All concerned with the album went on to great futures in music, none more so than Fiachra Trench who was responsible for many "High Energy" dance hits in the late 70s and early 80s. His later work concentrated on musical scores for Movies such as Die Hard and Pearl Harbour.

Containing three hit singles, two well produced cover versions and plenty of easy to listen to pop tracks the album eventually sold enough to go gold in the UK, despite never spending a day on the LP chart. This was mainly down to the continuous sales generated via constant singles success in the coming years.

# All the Ladies Laughing Gaily

"Poppa Joe" was the record that saved The Sweet from an early grave.

Had it not been for Chinn and Chapman's second foray into the land of limbo dancing and steel drums the entire pop landscape of the decade could have looked very different. Backed on the b-side with a real Connolly sing along number called 'Jeanie', 'Poppa Joe' pulled The Sweet kicking and screaming back to the top end of the UK charts.

This was the moment the real metal of Chinn and Chapman was to be tested, could they pull the relatively un established act back from a critically worthy but commercially blind alley. 'Poppa Joe's peak of number eleven and the Silver Disc it earned all said yes.

When performing the song on Top of the pops all four of them really went for it, the costumes were ultra bright and Brian's hair was bleached to a new level of blondness. Off screen Mick proudly paraded his latest T-shirt that sported the words "four hit wonders"

'Poppa Joe' was a huge hit throughout northern Europe keeping Sweet's publicists at Tony Barrow enterprises very busy supplying photo's and stories to the worlds press. Two people in particular were closely involved, Maureen O'Grady and Norman

Divall. Maureen had been press officer for The Rolling Stones and at her instigation the band very publicly supported their bubble gum image and sound. Her policy was " at least be seen to believe in what you are doing" Barrow had an office in Hanover St London where the band would meet to do interviews with magazines such a Jackie and Mirabel. Brian became almost a daily visitor to the offices as more and more the papers and magazines wanted the blond one, the lead singer, the Star!

Brian was now a recognisable figure almost everywhere he went and one member of the band in particular was not happy with all the attention he was getting.

Most bubble gum hits were being performed by acts cobbled together by canny producers. The Archies, singers of the multi million selling 'Sugar Sugar' didn't actually exist at all. In the case of the Sweet there certainly was a real band behind the image but the music required a pin up to sell it and Brian fitted the bill in spades.

With 'Poppa Joe' climbing the charts at breakneck speed all over the world Brian took the plunge and married long time sweetheart Marilyn on 7th March 1972. The event made national news causing some concern within the Sweet camp; would a married Brian still be acceptable as a teen idol?

# Little Willy big in America!

**At** this point in their careers as song writers Chinn and Chapman had done rather well. Along with the four hits enjoyed by Sweet the pair had also provided a further three for a trio called New World.

New World had won a UK TV talent contest called Opportunity Knocks, hosted by TV legend Hughie Green. After their initial success with a cover of the song 'Rose Garden' the future looked uncertain, as is often the case with acts whose big break comes via a talent show. Chinn and Chapman furnished the trio with four chart singles in all, the biggest being the ballad 'Tom Tom Turnaround' and the bubble gum classic 'Sister Jane' in 1972. All members of Sweet resented the fact that Chinn and Chapman's magic wand worked equally well when waved in other directions.

'Little Willy' flew into the UK chart in June 1972 peaking at number four, similar success repeated itself all over Europe, in Germany the song went to the very top of the chart for several weeks.

Like the previous four RCA hits, Sweet did not play the instruments on 'Little Willy'.

While it is true that many acts of the day did not have the skill or talent to play on their own records, there are many other reasons for the employment of session players in the studios of that era. Certainly in Sweet's case there was no shortage of either talent or skill, the reason was purely down to issues of control and money. Phil Wainman was as bad as Chinn and Chapman in this respect, all three knew that seasoned session men could knock out a Sweet hit in no time and would play it in the exact way they were told to. On the B-sides the band were given a free hand and once again Sweet returned to a heavy rock sound on the flip side of 'Little Willy'. The song 'Man From Mecca' was written in response to the Mecca ballroom giants who had blocked Sweet performing any more shows at their venues. Sweet's act was deemed "to lewd and suggestive" as the band were apt to play about quite a bit with the young girls in the audience and also made suggestive gestures with their hands when trying out the newly written 'Little Willy'. Although the b-side was called 'Man from Mecca' it doesn't seem to have any lyrical comment to make on the situation so it seems likely that the title was given after the song was recorded.

'Little Willy' was the first Sweet single that could realistically have been played by the band, they could not have been expected to play half of the instruments used on 'Alexander Graham Bell' and 'Co Co' as they were "exotics" and mood creators such horns, strings and Caribbean Steel drums. Like wise no one would have expected newly recruited guitarist Andy Scott to play piano on 'Funny Funny'. Though 'Little Willy' actually sounds like more of a band effort, Sweet do not play anything on the recording, Phil Wainman played the drums in addition to producing the record, while the guitar work is provided by Pip Williams. Williams had now played on all five RCA singles and Andy Scott found this particularly intolerable. Williams was guitarist of choice for many pop producers as he was super talented and ultra reliable. This was perfectly fine for the likes of the New Seekers and New World but Sweet were now out growing the over controlling ways of Chinnichap and Wainman.

The chance to prove their point came by way of a change in the rules laid down by the musicians union. As it was impossible to re create the actual sound of a hit record in a TV studio most acts simply mimed. In May 1972 the musicians union decreed that original recordings could not be mimed to on TV. For many pop acts and solo singers this meant re recording their hits with TV studio musicians, thus ensuring that the union members would still get their fees. The Sweet simply went into their regular recording studio and in three hours not only re created 'Little Willy' but considerably improved upon it. It was their version that was heard on TV to promote the song and from now on Pip and his pals would be backing other acts. Indeed Pip Williams went on to become a top producer working for many years with Status Quo.

Brain's fame was now in the super league, girls screamed, Marilyn bit her lip and Mick Tucker had yet another T-shirt made, however all was not peace and light within the Sweet.

Andy was beginning to resent Brian's ever increasing popularity, Brian would report to Hanover square on almost a daily basis and be dispatched to a photo shoot or go up stairs to the interview suite to meet the press. Even if the entire band were present it was Brian that the lenses and microphones were after. Though frequently hung over from the previous nights partying he seemed to thrive on it all. Andy complained bitterly to all who would listen at Tony Barrow but when push came to shove he was not half as keen to indulge the press in the same way that Brian did. Maureen at the agency sat him down and explained that while it would always be Brian who got the bulk of the attention she would be able in time to boost the other members profiles, with that she promptly found him and Mick some interviews with music papers such as Disc and Record week. Brian's image continued to cover the walls of a million bedrooms around the world.

Success in the US was terribly important in the early 1970s. During the pre Pop Video and MTV era, concerts and live TV appearances were all an act had as tools to promote its product. In the UK there was Top Of The Pops, watched by tens of millions each week. If you looked good and made an impact on that show your career was off to a good start. Some fifteen months earlier Brian Connolly had done just that while performing 'Funny Funny'.

In America it was vastly different, many times bigger than the UK, occupying a whole continent; it was not possible to crack America with radio plays alone. The Ed Sullivan Show was certainly a mark of industry approval in those days but to penetrate America took many months of touring and promotion.

'Little Willy', by the Sweet, a British domestic pop act from Ruislip, so named because they used to rehearse above a Sweet shop in Harlesden North London, who didn't actually play on the record as there was no money to correct mistakes, reached number THREE in the USA. For some uncanny reason Americans fell in love with 'Little Willy', which became forever more Sweet's biggest US hit. Although there was talk of a tour it was far too early in the game to send a group with one hit across the world while in Europe they were literally number one.

# Wig Wam Bam
## (Romantically Speaking)

It is only with the gift of hindsight that the full extent of Chinn and Chapman's genius becomes apparent; in September 1972 they had already showed fantastic promise. 'Wig Wam Bam', the first single on which Sweet played all the instruments, was another perfect star vehicle. This was the special ingredient, the Chinnichap factor at play. When writing for their teeny bop audience the pair really got under the skin of a pubescent child's psyche. 'Wig Wam Bam' was a solid building block in Sweet's career progression, providing an incredibly commercial platform for the emerging musicianship on the bands records. Having played on the TV version of 'Little Willy' there was no going back for Sweet. 'Little Willy' had also been a turning point in the bands image, particularly Steve Priest's. He had been sharing dressing room corridors with the likes of Marc Bolan and David Bowie and could smell a new trend in the air. Glam Rock as it would be known was in its infancy when Steve first donned a pair of spangled hot pants on Top Of The Pops. No doubt about it there he was in April 1972 cross dressing for the whole world to see. Brian was also covered in make up but it was standard camouflage to improve his looks on camera, with Steve it was a different story altogether! For 'Wig Wam Bam' the entire group went the whole hog and pushed the boundaries of good taste to breaking point-silver hot pants with tassels for Steve, huge earrings for Mick and an outrageous Indian headdress for Andy. Covered in lipstick and mascara the four of them later described themselves as mincing old whores. Publicly they continued to obey Maureen's advice and "revel" in their growing notoriety; privately they were a little humiliated by it all.

The probable reason for the artists' dislike of these numbers is most evident in the performing of them. Not many folks will have the opportunity to stand before a thousand people attempting to convey the words;

Wig Wam Bam gonna make you my man
Wam Bam Bam gonna get you if I can
Wig Wam Bam gonna make you understand
Try a little touch, try a little too much
Try a little Wig Wam Bam

They were perfect pop singles, superb dance along party records but in a concert setting they really had to be delivered as performance art
Or else things could feel a little embarrassing.

Over the decades commentators both within and outside the Sweet's camp have either ridiculed or some how tried to excuse the likes of 'Little Willy' and 'Wig Wam Bam', even Phil Wainman in 2005 declared that the song wasn't exactly "a milestone in musical history".

'Wig Wam Bam' was a work of genius because it made rock stars out of a band seen as little more than a novelty bubble gum pop group who had been very lucky. They had at last walked through the door from bubblegum to rock music though it was still at the most commercial end of the spectrum.

With 13 weeks in the UK chart, a Gold and Silver disc to its credit and three weeks at number one in Germany, 'Wig Wam Bam' will forever be one of the pivotal moments in Sweet's recording history.

Andy was by now incensed with the disparity between his and Brian's fame. Brian was now in need of protection on the streets of Germany and at home in the UK, his face was everywhere to be seen in a newsagent shop. It seemed a formula had arrived, Connolly on the cover and "one of the others" on page six by the cross word, perhaps telling the reader about why they loved their favourite food.

Andy nicknamed the band "Ruby and the Romantics", Brian being the offending Ruby, the rest of them being simply Brian's backing band. The others did not feel half so put out about Brian's popularity and so a rift began to develop between lead singer and lead guitarist.

They were now living in the fast lane and the pressure was increasing by the day. Chinn was out of his depth with regard to managing a growing global phenomenon and frequently planned tours that were punishing purely because of poor scheduling. Brian, always a heavy drinker and smoker used booze and fags to get him through the ordeal, he smoked so many Benson and Hedges that his fingers were often stained with nicotine. He also began cheating on Marilyn his wife of less than a year. On one or two occasions he used Maureen and Norman at the agency as excuses for staying out all night, claiming that because there were early morning appointments he was staying the night on the pair's couches. Once she found out about this deception Maureen told Brian in no uncertain terms that if he did it again she would squeal. "I thought Marilyn was a lovely girl and while we turned a blind eye to a lot of things I was not going to be party to his cheating on her" she confided in 2007. Marilyn has stated publicly that what she didn't see she didn't care about but that was no doubt a very brave face for the cameras. Looking at it from the bands point of view, it would be a very strong willed young man in his twenties that could refuses the dozens of advances per day from some very pretty young girls. It was 'Crazy' that they had gotten married in the first place but again Marilyn was a young girl with a long term partner who had gone and become a "rock star" these were unique circumstances that few would know how to cope with, especially when so young. In November Andy threatened to leave the band for no better reason than his hatred of their silly songs and his jealousy of Brian. Things were hastily smoothed over, as always there was simply too much at stake, they had a greatest hits album to promote. Sweet's biggest hits was released at least a year too soon and failed to make the charts. Instead of a celebration of the bubble gum era it was seen by the band more as a sort of trunk in which to dump yesterdays fashion disasters. At the time commentators quipped that it was a little premature to release a greatest hits, especially as the band had not put out an album that year containing original material. The album naturally sold bucket loads in Germany and Scandinavia where most of the singles had been number ones. Its failure in the UK was quickly forgotten after Chinn and Chapman had played the band the demo for the next single, this one really did sound like something entirely different.

# Blockbuster

**There** are books, there are films and there are simply moments that herald a significant change or the start of an era. It has been commented on more than one occasion that the siren at the start of 'Blockbuster' signalled such a change; indeed some have said that it was the true start of the 1970s.

Although David Bowie had released 'The Jean Genie' some three weeks ahead of Sweet, using an identical chord structure and similar sound, 'Blockbuster' was the tune that totally captured the British spirit of Glam Rock at that exact moment. To an American the phrase Block Buster simply means a bomb capable of destroying a whole street, 'Blockbuster' the song failed to excite the Americans and peaked at number seventy three. This was in part due to the removal of the iconic siren at the start of the record, the authorities believed it might cause panic in public areas such as shopping malls. Another reason for the songs lowly placing stateside was that it was used as a follow up to 'Little Willy' not 'Wig Wam Bam', Chinnichap's conveyor belt product was made in such a way that each fitted together in a perfect progression. The jump from 'Little Willy' to 'Blockbuster' was, in terms of style, huge and it left the Yanks simply confused as to what the Sweet was all about. To those in most other countries, not least the UK 'Blockbuster' is the song that crystallized the moment that we said goodbye to the swinging sixties. Nothing quite like it had been heard before. The elements that drove the song along were standard riffs and repeats used many times in American music, but it was the siren and the wail that to this day make it one of the most distinctive records ever released.

'Blockbuster' was created entirely for one purpose, to give Sweet a number one hit and that is exactly what it did. Within a few weeks of release the song was sitting proud at the top of the charts and Sweet's public acceptance went through the roof. Unlike Marc Bolan, whose career would slowly fade through 1973, Sweet soared into the most dizzying heights of pop superstardom, all because of a siren and a wail.

As 'Blockbuster' began to slide from the top of the chart it collided with a number called 'Crazy' by a new group called MUD. MUD's record had the words Chinn/Chapman under the title, it seemed that Batman and Robin had done it again. Although Sweet had actually introduced this new group to their mentors they were very unhappy with the growing Chinnichap phenomenon. It was a simple case of envy, the bigger their writers became and the more acts they propelled into he chart, the less "special" Sweet would appear to be.

Financially 'Blockbuster' took them all into another league; Brian sold the Ford Capri and invested in a Rolls Royce, then a Mercedes to keep it company. Although Sweet played on 'Blockbuster' and had a lot to do with the arrangement, Mike Chapman's controlling ways overcame him and he wiped off Andy's acoustic guitar track and replaced it with his own. It seems he had sensed that this single would literally become a 'Blockbuster' and he wanted to be able to say he had played on it. Andy Scott was furious, perhaps justifiably so.

It was about this time that the press began to de construct the myth surrounding Brian's age. He was twenty-eight but claimed to have recently turned twenty-three. Despite the press being fed literally hundreds of versions of his life, most told of adoption and the merchant navy in the year 1963. If he were twenty-three at the time of 'Blockbuster' he would have joined the Merchant navy at the rather tender age of thirteen!

# Honeysuckle Burning in the Fires of Hell

**By** the time Sweet's eighth smash hit was released they were becoming very upset by the trouncing they were getting in the music press. Mick begged Maureen to get them an interview with Julie Webb at NME but she and her colleagues at the paper had yet to see the light. While Brian was certainly not happy about this, his position as "King of the pin ups" at magazines like Jackie and Popswop had become undisputable.

Seven days after the release of 'Hell Raiser', Mick ordered his latest T-shirt; they were now eight hit wonders.

From the moment it begins it is quite clear that 'Hell Raiser' is going to be a musical roller coaster ride. "Look out!" screams Brian, then there is the explosion, possibly the most perfectly recorded explosion in pop history, followed curiously by a guitar played and produced to sound like a ticking bomb. 'Hell Raiser' is Rock n Roll having undergone a major refurbishment. The production really is unique on the record, very heavy toward the bass and the treble ends of the sound spectrum; Phil Wainman had outdone himself for the Sweet's eighth hit. After the release of 'Wig Wam Bam'

Mike Chapman had begun to impersonate Sweet on his demo recordings for the band. Having learned their vocal characteristics and ranges he structured everything around them. Steve's camp interjections were born because of a suggestion by Andy Scott. Brian was not at all happy to be sharing needle time with his bass player's vocals too. Though it caused some temporary friction, Andy's idea was a stroke of genius and the public loved the "poofy ones" cries of "We just haven't got a clue what to do" More and more the input from the band began to compliment the superb tunes dreamed up by Chinn and Chapman. Throughout 'Hell Raiser' the guitar is crisp and infectious yet never too heavy.

Of all Sweet's personnel Steve did *High Camp* the most convincingly. At this point in time almost every act appearing on BBC's Top Of The Pops was wearing Glam artefacts though Steve was probably the campest pop performer to appear on British Television. The Fan base was still too young to fully appreciate the full connotations of Steve's borderline cross-dressing or the utter *Queerness* of his performance. There was also a degree of crassness about Sweet's version of Glam rock, they were too straight to fully appreciate the "travesty" aspect of what they were doing, however this worked in their favour as a "joke" of this kind was acceptable on prime time TV. The Rocky Horror Show had just reached the London stage and was seen as quite disturbing because it simply featured freaks as characters rather than just poking fun at them.

Brian always maintained a veneer of reality about his performance, a certain degree of integrity, while Steve went for total all out Pantomime. This was a very good strategy, as lead singer and pin up star Brian needed to carry the narrative of the material, no matter how macabre or surreal it was becoming. Steve loved the dressing up; all who knew him at the time agree he loved the make up and the costumes.

The band members themselves, with the exception of Connolly, have all left on record remarks that would land them in hot water with the politically correct lobby, or indeed simply the general public of this century. In a truly dire interview in 1972 poor Steve is forced to take part in dreadful anti gay humour, to say nothing of the mockery regarding their latest million selling hit 'Wig Wam Bam'.

Uniquely, the members of the Sweet all experienced the hurt of homophobic comment and discrimination, while actually being straight!

If that wasn't bad enough a young lady had not long stepped off a plane from Detroit USA and her producer Mickie Most had contacted Chinn and Chapman in the hope that they could kick start her career. Their answer was we certainly 'Can the Can' and within weeks the girl named Suzi was number one. MUD was also in the top twenty with their second hit Hypnosis. There could be no doubt about it, Brian and Sweet were part of a conveyor belt and they hated it. How were they ever going to be taken as seriously as Deep Purple or even Slade if their writers continued to make hit production look so easy!

The B-side 'Burning' is one of the legendary Sweet cuts, produced before the group Queen had even come into being. Recorded just after Christmas 72 and released with 'Hell Raiser' in the final week of April 73 'Burning' has many elements of what would become Queens first hit 'Seven Seas of Rye'. Slightly under produced because of financial considerations, Sweets early b-sides have a fresh and raw quality that still endears them today. Released some twenty months earlier, Lead Zeppelin's early work 'Immigrant Song' was obviously the inspiration for Sweet's b-side. Both songs feature a distinctive riff and the screaming layered harmonies that Queen would put to such good use. Considering the fact that 'Burning' was the product of a band that had just sung 'Little Willy' wont go home, it is quite remarkable.

# It Was Like Lightning

**'Ballroom Blitz'** was released on September 15th 1973 and was an immediate smash with the public worldwide. In the UK it quickly climbed to number two and was held off the top spot not by one but by two opponents in succession. 'See My Baby Jive' by Wizard and an unlikely orchestral hit called 'Eye Level' by Simon Park and his orchestra. The latter was the theme tune to a detective series called Vandervaulk and had been released twice before, suddenly at the end of 1973 it stormed the charts and prevented Sweet from enjoying a much deserved 2nd chart topper.

'Ballroom Blitz' is a wonderful record, much loved by many generations of pop fans, as always Phil Wainman had produced a polished and restrained sound with plenty of power. Chinn and Chapman had now written the Sweet three of the year's best tunes; each one could have launched the bands career from a standing point. There is little of anything new in the song it self, arranger Tony Hatch used similar chord repeats in several of his orchestral pop tunes during the 1960s.

Brian mixes his vocal style constantly flipping from an ultra effeminate whimper to screaming rock god, always with a high camp tongue in cheek attitude. He was becoming a little tired of singing not only Chinn and Chapman's pop hits but also heavy rock music in general. As a singer he was maturing and wanted material that he could put some genuine emotion into.

By now Brian was becoming quite wealthy on paper though his expenses were high, often due to Rock star extravagances. One of these was a boat on the River Thames in Surrey, he had loved the sea since his days in the Navy and spent what little spare time he had ploughing up and down the river on his motor cruiser. This made for some great publicity photos but just as when he had married, the PR people were not at all convinced that another development in his life would be good for business, Marylyn was pregnant. Although this development did have the potential to tarnish his pop idol credentials, Sweet were now at a point in their career where almost nothing could stop the momentum.

It is hard to imagine the depth of talent possessed by Chinn and Chapman at this point in musical history. Their chart output was now constant. 'Blockbuster' in January, 'Crazy' in March, 'Hell Raiser' in April, 'Can the Can' in May, 'Hypnosis' in June and 'Ballroom Blitz' in September, followed by 'Daytona Demon' in October. Sweet, Suzi Quattro and MUD were now among Europe's biggest selling acts. New World had been dropped earlier in the year after the public's interest had waned.

Frustrating though it must have been for the Chinnichap acts whose own material was confined to the b sides and album tracks, it is inconceivable that any of them could have matched the uniquely successful songwriters abilities in producing classic hits.

The B-side of 'Ballroom Blitz' finds Sweet making fun of the whole situation with the song 'Rock and Roll Disgrace'. 'Ballroom Blitz' marked the highest point of regard for the band in the UK and Europe. Throughout the year Brian had mentioned in interviews that the band were in the process of recording an album that traced the history of rock and roll from the fifties, through to the late seventies. There was some excitement in the press regarding what type of sound would be used to represent the "future" in the case of the late seventies numbers. Because of Chinn's erratic tour scheduling and the constant demands of TV promotion the band never really completed the album. Chinn and Chapman were the ultimate hit merchants with regard singles but on the album front they had less to offer. Brian seemed very keen on the rock n roll album while Andy was totally dismayed by the idea. In the event Chinn and Chapman went to America on a talent scouting mission and the project was taken over by Phil Wainman. Over the Christmas period Brian found a house in Gerrards Cross for him and his growing family to live in. All four members of the band now owned homes in the north London stock broker belt, this was ironic as financially they were not being well managed or well advised. Chinn and Chapman's income was off the dial at the close of 1973, in this their ultimate year they had scored ten hits, two of which had hit number one, they had started the year as just millionaires but finished it as multimillionaires, since 1971 they had enjoyed nineteen hits in total. Sweet had been a large part of that success and Brian was a quarter of the Sweet which meant that his fortune was way below that of Chinn and Chapman's. This did not stop his extravagances; indeed all four members of the band were slowly leaving the confines of the real world behind.

# There's Something in the Air

**Toward** the close of 1973 Mike Chapman presented Sweet with his demo for their next single. 'Dyna Mite' was an excellent song, very Sweet sounding and ultra commercial. Brian and Steve were happy enough with it while Andy and Mick were adamant; they thought it rubbish and a real step backward musically. After nine huge hits Brian and co were beginning to have some clout with Chapman who, sensing that he wouldn't win a stand off, capitulated returning forty eight hours later with a replacement song. Not much longer than forty-eight hours after that MUD were in the studio recording 'Dyna Mite' for themselves. Their label had a slot for a single all ready planned for them, it was a Chinnichap number called Moonshine Sally, which was shelved in place of Sweet's "cast-off". This allowed MUD to release 'Dyna Mite' at the close of 1973 and enjoy their biggest hit so far, a number four. Suddenly MUD was very hot indeed and Chinn and Chapman sensed that a peak could be hit if they delivered the right song after the Christmas holidays. 'Teenage Rampage' was now in the bag and RCA had it scheduled for a January release. Knowing that timing is every thing to a number one single Chinn and Chapman allowed Mickie Most's RAK label to go head to head with Sweet and in February 1974 Sweet were knocked back into second place by a song they probably should have had for themselves. 'Tiger Feet' sold millions around the world and was indeed the pinnacle of MUD's career. Mick Tucker described it as a dreadful song, which really demonstrated his total lack of "ear for a hit". Brian would often joke that MUD only recorded Sweet's cast off's but again it is ironic that he could not see that Dyna mite was the song that really pushed MUD to the fore and into a position to have a number one hit with 'Tiger Feet'. Despite 'Teenage Rampage' being an instant smash, reaching the familiar number two spot and attaining gold status, the song is, compared to the previous five releases, just more of the same. The growth so apparent from 'Little Willy' to 'Ballroom Blitz' is not there on 'Teenage Rampage', which also lacked the humour of 'Dyna Mite' and thus never quite became a true Sweet classic.

Brian found the song problematic to sing as it really was little more than screaming at times. Also he was pushing thirty and his late nights and heavy smoking were taking a toll on his voice. He was not alone; the entire band was indulging in excessive drinking and partying. Even Andy who was by nature a home bird was now caught up in the rock and roll life style. This didn't help the situation between him and Brian, it seemed to him that he wrote the songs while Brian introduced them to the press and took the credit for them. The songs had been mainly b-sides up to this point, though this was about to change. A huge change that had already occurred at the end of 1973 was the sacking of Nicky Chinn as Sweet's manager. From October onward they had decided that they could manage themselves. This was by no means a healthy situation and was seen as temporary but Chinn plainly hadn't had the experience to control the monster he had created. The Sweet was massively successful in the UK but that was nothing compared to the record-breaking superstardom they had seen in Europe. 'Teenage Rampage' became Sweet's sixth single to reach number one in Germany.

It wasn't all glitz and glamour though and there was a serious downside to all of the camping it up.

One evening out at a local club in Hayes, Middlesex, Brian landed in trouble with some lads he had seen by the bar. There are many versions of the events that night so it will never be possible to know the exact truth. Possibly he tried to steal their girlfriends or they accused him of being "queer" or it was an act of pure jealousy, one thing is certain, that night would have an effect on Brian for the rest of his life. He claims that as he left the bar he was confronted by three lads who were jumping on the roof of his Mercedes. He told the press that after he challenged them the youths attacked, forcing him to the ground, deliberately kicking him in the throat. This was the one irrevocable fact in the story; he was badly beaten and definitely kicked many times in the head and throat. For anyone this would be a terrible trauma to cope with but for a rock singer with his vocal commitments it was a catastrophe. For a start he had to finish recording the long awaited Sweet album and then there would be a lengthy tour to promote it. Sweet FA as it was first called was no longer the history of Rock n Roll. Now it was to be the Sweet's showcase, a work to take on tour to show the world that it had been very wrong, Sweet were the real thing, a Rock Band of distinction. Behind the scenes many people were becoming bowled over by the bands incredible metamorphoses, not least members of the Who. So impressed were they that they asked the band to open for them at Charlton Athletic football club. This really was a chance to stand up and be counted right next to the big boys, the Who were legends in Rock and they wanted to share a stage with The Sweet. As the time grew nearer for the show it became clear that Brian's voice was not recovering from the beating. He also had to let Steve priest take the lead vocals on several tracks on the new album. Steve obliged gladly and gave the best performances of his career despite the keys being way above his usual range. The club where Brian had been attacked was not the sort of haunt that one would find a millionaire rock star in and by now Brian was simply too famous, not to mention notorious to have hung out un protected in such a place. When the time came to announce the cancellation of the Who show, Brian was beside himself with feelings of humiliation. Andy was just plain furious with Brian, even in the press he let slip that it was unwise for his comrade to have been drinking alone in Hayes of all places. Despite a year of superstardom the members of Sweet were considered to be that "mad bunch of poofters" from the telly, adored by their teenage audience but much maligned among working class men in pubs and bars. Because of Brian's error of judgment Andy was going to miss his chance to rock with The Who. The moment, their moment was beginning to pass and such an opportunity would not arise again.

**One of Cos Cinnino's infamous collages from the Fan Club**

# Sweet Fanny Adams

**While** on one hand the singles career of Sweet had been managed and guided perfectly some pretty glaring mistakes were made with regard album releases. Sweet FA was deemed by RCA to be unacceptable as a title because of its connotation with a four letter word. Sweet Fanny Adams was for some reason deemed to be appropriate.

Prior to the release of Sweet Fanny Adams the band had released only Sweet's Biggest hits and the premier offering Funny How Sweet 'Co Co' can be. The biggest hits album had been far too early while Sweet Fanny Adams was a little late.

Sweet Fanny Adams is almost certainly the Sweet at their peak, it is a wonderful combination of out right pop tunes and much more subtle rock works, the term under rated could have been invented for Sweet Fanny Adams. Unstoppable as they were abroad it was no surprise to see the album make the top ten across northern Europe and top the chart in Germany. At home in the UK it was another matter, Sweet's finest hour and one of Rocks best early albums peaked at a lowly number twenty seven.

Had it been marketed differently, put out with six tracks per side instead of just four and included the previous three singles it would have been a perfect record to release at the end of 1973. Obviously an alternate version of the album would have begun with 'Blockbuster' and 'Ballroom Blitz' and then settled into cuts from the LP. Side Two would perhaps have begun with 'Hell Raiser' and continued with the heavier material from the set.

By Christmas 1973 The Sweet were enjoying fame known to only a select few, it was hysteria, with market penetration on all levels. Key rings, carrier bags, pens, pencil cases, scarves, hats and posters. They had been in the UK singles chart for one and one half years with no breaks; in 1973 alone Sweet had spent 35 weeks in the chart, 14 of which were at either number one or number two. Despite this truly phenomenal success no album was released in their finest hour.

When it did appear in 1974 Sweet Fanny Adams did nowhere near as well as it should. This was largely because the bands following were singles buyers and none of the singles were included on the album. The album does contain several of Sweets best compositions, produced beautifully by Phil Wainman. The pop numbers are solid enough to appeal to older students and adults, the rock numbers restrained enough to keep the kids on board.

'Heartbreak Today' demonstrates the true talents of Steve Priest in sharing a lead vocal with Brian Connolly. Musically it is faultless.

'Set Me Free' delivers the decibels for the fans of a heavy rock Sweet, yet the piece is restrained and remains integrated rather than just a platform for guitar solos. 'Rebel Rouser' sees Sweet flirting with the idea of a self-written pop single and it is perfectly plausible that 'Rebel Rouser' could have scored very high.

'Peppermint Twist' is a perfectly rendered version of an old Joe Dee song from many years before and while not out of place on the album it is not necessary, all Sweets recent hits were missing and adding a Rock and Roll cover was more in keeping with the style of a MUD LP. Later in the year while on tour in Australia RCA put out 'Peppermint Twist' as a single, it topped the chart there for two weeks making it Sweet's only "cover version" single.

'Restless' is another example of perfect production and excellent song writing, tough in his autobiography "Ready Steve" Priest owns up to stealing the idea for the song from Elvis Presley's 'Heartbreak Hotel'. It is abundantly clear from the material released on Sweet Fanny Adams that the Sweet was an exceptionally talented band who's songs when produced correctly were a perfect compliment to Chinn and Chapman's hit singles.

'ACDC' was one of the best Chinnichap tunes "never" to have been a UK single. Naughty, fun, fast paced yet just a little more adult in style and lyric, it would have been a smash hit while also appealing to the more mature psyche of the nation. If, being a song about a bisexual lady, the BBC had banned it so what! It was the kind of saucy number that would probably have sold even more.

Sweet Fanny Adams embraced a sound and a style that would have served the band well for some time to come. This was in no small way because of the production skill of Phil Wainman, since 1968 he had loved and guided the Sweet, sometimes he was a little too controlling perhaps but of their total output of fifteen singles he had produced eleven and ten of those had been hits.

# Life Goes On...
# But it Ain't Easy After Wainman

**Inside** every band there are tensions, musical, egotistical, artistic or simply tensions created out of desires to control. One casualty of the latter was Phil Wainman. First Chinn was ousted as manager, then in early 1974 Phil Wainman was fired as producer. Chinn's demise came as a direct order from the band, Wainmans's more by the instigation of Chinn and Chapman. Phil had produced the groups every hit for three years and their three album releases too. His trick was to provide a commercially acceptable sound for the singles and this he did perfectly. He had no great pretensions musically and saw Sweet as a long-term project, perhaps maturing into a more laid back country rock and blues outfit. He certainly realised quite quickly that newcomers Queen were going to steel Sweet's thunder in the rock harmony genre. Only Steve was keen to follow his suggestion, Andy and Mick were still craving heavy Rock superiority. Strangely, so too were Chinn and Chapman. Mainly it was Mike Chapman who became tempted by the bands promise of rock credibility on a plate. Perhaps he himself could become seen as legit if Sweet turned the heavy rock corner. Not content with the sweeping changes of management and production Sweet also severed ties with Tony Barrow enterprises and thus lost their trusty Maureen and Norman as press officers. These two had worked tirelessly to ensure that Sweet were in the kids magazines constantly. Stories were beefed up or simply invented by Maureen and disseminated to the press for consumption. On one occasion she had written a fictitious column for Mirabel magazine where Brian and Steve told of getting lost on the New York Subway while on tour in the US. Mirabel needed copy six weeks ahead of publication so when the tour was cancelled right at the last minute nothing could be done to stop Brian and Steve describing in detail a place that they had never set foot in. Crass, crazy or just plain silly Barrow's press machine had served Sweet well and they were going to miss it sorely.

Following the ousting of Phil Wainman as producer Chinn and Chapman set forth believing they would create a new beginning for Sweet.

Phil Wainman had always capped the excesses and noisiness of Scott's guitar work in the studio, Chinn and Chapman now indulged in it. First up was the single 'The Sixteens', there were several forces at play at this time including Brian's wish to sing something more meaningful and heartfelt. Having been the founding member of a pop-folk outfit in the late 60s he had somehow spent the last two years belting and screaming glam rock and heavy metal. Ironically the Connolly screech was to become considered one of the great rock voices of the era, he had helped create a style of rock singing he hadn't even intended to pursue.

Unlike much later guitar bands, the MUDs', Sweets' and Slades' were designed for fun and were rarely off the turntable at a family party or disco.

'The Sixteens' was a total departure from this genre. It was too slow to dance to and too noisy to appeal to the general public.

The release peaked at Number 9 in the UK and saw Sweet sharing a week on the chart with Queen for the first time. Phil Wainman had been right, he had heard it on Queen's first album, Sweet had opened the door but Freddie and co would be the ones to walk right through it.

'Seven Seas of Rye' had marked the arrival of a new band that sounded uncannily like Sweet on their previous b-sides, b-sides released before Mercury and his musicians had made a sound.

The Queen record contained subtleties and stylish frills that Sweet had not yet tried on a single, yet at the same time the record was exciting and appealing to youngsters who had been fed on a diet of full throttle glam for the previous three years. 'The Sixteens' got very good reviews in the press but was not so popular with Sweet's fans, in Germany it broke the spell and ended a run of six consecutive number ones.

At the time Brian declared that he was happier to be at number nine with a good record than at number one or two some commercial rubbish. This was not good practise, knocking your previous stock and the people who had bought it. Critics were united in their praise for the record, almost all citing it as the best Chinn/Chapman song ever. In truth it was too noisy and sluggish to be a single and only charted as high as it did because of the previous recording successes.

'The Sixteens' was part of the Desolation Boulevard album, the first album not to be produced by Wainman. With MUD and Suzi Quattro still topping the singles chart Mike Chapman now saw Sweet as his passport to credibility. 'The Sixteens' had not quite hit the mark so it was decided to go for a second album in the autumn of 1974. This was a crazy idea as Sweet Fanny Adams was less than six months old. The Sweet was big yes but it would be a very big act indeed that could shift two LPs in less than one year. Although the songs were recorded in a more natural way Brian still had problems hitting the higher notes when doing lead vocals. In the six months since the attack he had rested to some degree but he had continued to smoke and nothing could stop him drinking. This combination plus continued work had left his voice permanently strained. Chapman was not making a highly polished album and did nothing to disguise Brian's raspy performance. In general the sound on the album is raw yet thin compared to the bands earlier material and this factor alone would limit its appeal. In America the groups label Capitol decided to cherry pick a couple of tracks from each of the year's albums and add their latest hit 'Ballroom Blitz'. This version did rather well in the states but did nothing to introduce the audience to most of Sweet's album material. Without Tried and trusted PR coverage or any really commercial songs on it Desolation Boulevard failed to chart in the UK. In Germany it was a top ten album but it was becoming clear that Sweet's golden moment was passing.

# For God's Sake 'Turn It Down'

**'Turn It Down'** was the absolute Nadir of Sweet's association with Chinn And Chapman, it was they're lowest selling UK single spending two weeks in the chart and peaking at an embarrassing Number 41.
The embarrassment stemming from the fact that the UK s premier singles band could release such an obvious dud.

It is said that the BBC banned the song because of the term "for god's sake 'Turn It Down'" but the harshness of the sound and length of the guitar solos combined with a total lack of "lift" on the chorus meant that ban or no ban it was unlikely to have been a hit.

'Turn It Down' was ignored by commercial stations and TV alike and seen as a wrong turn, rather than creative exhaustion.

It was so unlike Chinn and Chapman to get it so wrong, they had tampered with their own brand and the public were voting with their feet. Brian was not at all happy with this choice of single as he thought that it "didn't have enough go in it". What it didn't have was anything Sweet about it, when one listens to the demo recording of the song played on an acoustic guitar the entire nature of the number changes, suddenly it becomes apparent that it was a nod toward Mick Jagger's territory. Chapman had not impersonated Sweet when writing the song but rather The Rolling Stones. This had not translated to the record; which was far too heavy to be a single without the relief of the demo versions acoustic guitar feel. In Germany it staggered to number four as had 'The Sixteens' but it fell back rather quicker and was soon forgotten.

Publicly, at the time Sweet pretended that the flop had never occurred. During a TV phone in on Sally James's program Saturday scene in March 75 the bands stance was that they had not made a record for a while. All went well till a fan asked why Brian thought that 'Turn It Down' had flopped.

"Ah, very smart of you, not many people know about that one, well we didn't really think it had enough "go" in it, not really" was his swift response to the caller who had undone the PR fabrication at a stroke.

Privately the band were reeling, they had started 1974 as pop superstars and were ending it unable to penetrate the top forty. The magazines no longer queued up for Brian to be on the cover and booking agents were not keen on financing a UK tour.

Forced into a corner by a band wishing for an ever-heavier image and now working without the producer who had helped create the bands optimum sound, Chinn and Chapman had served up a total dud. One of the few other times they would turn a blind alley was with a song for Suzi Quattro called 'Your Mamma Won't Like Me' which once again left the confines of a pop formula in an effort to transform Suzi into a disco diva. That effort fared a little better at Number 35. Both numbers fail to run true as works by the artists who delivered them, many a Sweet fan may disagree, however both singles failed mid way through an otherwise unbroken string of hits for the writers and artists concerned. As Brian and Marilyn prepared for the birth of their first child he speculated as to whether the little one would ever see its father on TV or in the charts. None of the band had ever speculated that Sweet would last longer than ten years and they were now well past the half way mark if that assertion were to come true.

Despite having some quiet time over the Christmas holidays Brian refused to take it easy. He had always drank to excess even as a lad in the merchant navy but increasingly he was finding time on his hands and could be found in his local pub in Gerrards Cross as early as twelve noon, sometimes not leaving for hours. Booze and fags may not have been particularly healthy but in the coming year all of the band would discover new ways to burn the candle at both ends.

# The
## Fox On The Run
### Phenomenon

**There** are certain records that have the smell of success almost imprinted in their grooves and 'Fox On The Run' was one of them. Brian loved the song, having fully participated in its composition he was over the moon when a record company executive suggested that the band use it as their first self penned single. Chinn and Chapman were not happy at all and claimed to know nothing about Sweet's decision to issue a non-Chinnichap song.

While it may be true that the band had not phoned them and discussed the matter, there were press reports at the time of 'The Sixteens' and 'Turn It Down' that clearly stated that a self written single was imminent.

'Fox On The Run' started life on the Desolation Boulevard album but the single version was a total re recording of the song.

The difference in how it was originally recorded and as it re appeared on March 15th is a classic demonstration of the importance of both arrangement and production when singles are concerned.

Version one is seen as little more than a demo compared to the sparkling classic that hit the charts in the spring of 1975.

Parting company with the unstoppable genius of Chinn and Chapman seemed all the more plausible after the terrible failure of 'Turn It Down'. It was something the band had aspired to from the very beginning, to write and produce its own singles and albums.

As early as May 1971 Brian told an interviewer for Disc magazine that the band were very happy with their first hit 'Funny Funny' but they would not rest until they had written a hit of their own. It had taken them another four years to pluck up the courage to go it alone.

The key problem in this plan was the fact that a single in the 1970s was no mere song, not simply the best track off an album. Nicky Chinn and Mike Chapman had made hand crafted vehicles for their artists with a skill rarely seen before or since. At the point where 'Turn It Down' failed for Sweet in October 1974 Chinn and Chapman were in fact at the peak of their powers.

The year had begun with 'Teenage Rampage' for Sweet reaching number two, held off the top spot by 'Tiger Feet' by MUD, both Chinn and Chapman compositions. With both songs still riding high in the charts Suzi Quattro hit the top spot in February with 'Devil Gate Drive'. Not content with a stable of three acts Chinn and Chapman then took on an act fronted by American songster Alan Merril, the result was a smash hit called 'Touch Too Much' for his group the Arrows. In total Chinn and Chapman wrote eleven top forty records in 1974 three of which reached number one. Leaving such a stable of guaranteed winners would have been an act of extreme bravery or mind blowing stupidity, had it not been for the failure of 'Turn It Down'.

Sweet's quest for heavy metal respectability had been relentless, relentless to the point that Chinn and Chapman had found themselves trying to write in a musical style that was not their forte.

When Sweet released 'Fox On The Run' on March 15th 1975 it was without the permission of their svengali songwriters. Chinn and Chapman had made them the stars they were and they were not pleased.

'The Sixteens' had underperformed, 'Turn It Down' had flopped, perhaps, just perhaps they really did have what it took; maybe they would be better off writing and producing for themselves. In recent interviews Nicky Chinn has stated that, had things been different, the band could have come to an arrangement where Sweet would write some of its singles while Chinn and Chapman would write others. This seems most unlikely, historically the pair controlled the singles output of their acts with an iron will. After all, why should they write an act into pop superstardom only to have the career progression corrupted by the ego emissions of those whose skill could never live up to the Chinnichap phenomenon. Why get a band or singer all the way to number two or three, ready for a 'Blockbuster' or 'Tiger Feet' only to see the impetus destroyed by the 'parasitic offerings' of their prodigies.

'Fox On The Run', had it appeared in place of 'The Sixteens' would almost certainly have made Number one in the UK, it really is one of the only Sweet self written singles to stand entirely on its own merit.

Chinn and Chapman however had the unique ability to start and re start the careers of the acts they controlled because, by and large, each song in some way stood on its own merit as a hit in its time.

For a few months in March, April and May of 19 75 it really did look as though something incredible was happening. 'Fox On The Run' out sold all the previous Sweet hits internationally and became the biggest seller of their career. All four members of the band were feeling particularly pleased with themselves and rather superior but this was only in part due to the success of their song.

Today in a world awash with illegal drugs it is hard to imagine that four young men in their position had hardly touched hard drugs by 1975. However back then in the UK and Europe it was probably harder for them to have found hard drugs than it would be for some school kids today. In his biography "Ready Steve" Priest describes the evening that he and Mick Tucker first tried cocaine and the feeling it produced. He tells of standing at a disco observing the revellers while feeling totally superior and detached.

Apparently a common feeling experienced by users of the drug one can only imagine its impact upon a wealthy rock star.

Very quickly the drug found a place within the band, so much so that by the next single Mick was wearing another kind of T shirt, one with the words "hit powder" written in jewels across the chest.

Financially things were at last really taking off but the money seemed to be flying in all sorts of directions. They had found a new manager for the UK and a separate agent and manager for the US. Across the pond things were really looking up with 'Fox On The Run' following 'Ballroom Blitz' into the American top five. Ed Leffler arranged a series of tours for the group and also a trip to Japan where Sweet were peaking with 'Teenage Rampage'. Back in Europe David walker was taking care of operations. One thing was obvious to all, the bulk of the current success was linked to previously recorded Chinnichap material but Mike and Nicky no longer wanted to know, it was now time for Sweet to deliver the goods.

# Not Everybody Wants A Piece of the Action

**Following** the rampant success of 'Fox On The Run' would be a difficult task for the most seasoned of hit makers, songwriters or producers. For Brian, Andy, Steve and Mick it would prove impossible. Written mainly by Mick and Andy, 'Action' had great promise as a follow up to the global phenomenon that was 'Fox On The Run'.

Instead of following the theme of a very sing able chorus, bolstered by harmonies and melodies sung together, 'Action' went for a somewhat thinner, yet harder sound. The joy and effervescence evident through every second of sweet's first self-penned single was deliberately and catastrophically missing on 'Action'.

Steve did not have any trade mark interjections to sing which pleased Brian but otherwise Sweet's front man was not enamoured with the song. This was the first time they had written and produced material specifically for the singles market and they missed their mark quite considerably. The fault lay in the production rather than the song itself.

Although 'Action' did not go down so well in the UK or US it is worth noting that both the Swiss and Belgium's took it to their hearts and into their top tens' as did the Australians, where it got to number four. In Germany it was business as usual and the song flew up the chart stopping at number two.

Despite all the foreign success 'Action' marked the end of Sweet's time as Britain's premier singles outfit. In Britain and the USA the single peaked at number fifteen loosing them thirteen places in the former country and ten in the latter. Critics liked the song and the new heavier sound of Sweet but critics are not the best judges of what makes a hit single, indeed they are frequently people who have failed as commercial musicians.

Although 'Fox On The Run' stood at the interface between rock and pop, it was still not out of place in a disco or party setting.

'Action', on the other hand was no dance hall favourite, the ferocity of Andy's guitar solo limited the songs appeal to those who appreciated heavy rock music.

Had 'Action' been produced by the capable hands of Phil Wainman It would no doubt have been less abrasive, far more tune full, while Andy's solo spot would have been easier on the ear.

Had Wainman produced the single it would have probably been longer, smoother, and made the top ten.

Queen had invaded Sweet's territory not by their hardness or heavy metal leanings but by cleverness and subtle innuendo in both lyric and musical style. Coming several years after Sweet they had had the opportunity to invent them selves at a point of the scenario that suited them. The bubble gum days were long over allowing Queen straight into the world at the 'Blockbuster' stage of the game. Queen would never have to navigate a pop chart peppered with the likes of 'Chirpy Chirpy Cheep Cheep' or 'Sugar Sugar'.

While Sweet's tentacles were spreading internationally the days of Chinn's over ambitious tour scheduling were over and so Brian had ever increasing amounts of time on his hands. On the home front all looked grand on paper; Marilyn gave birth to a healthy baby girl who the couple named Nicola. Brian took up riding, keeping a horse at a nearby stable. He was still in great demand for promotional work in Germany, especially for magazines such as Bravo but his pin up days were numbered. This was in part because the music now flowing from the band was not of such interest to the readers of teen magazines and also because he was a man of thirty. Either way his position in the band was shifting, he took less and less part in the process of making the music, music that he was inclined to think was a bit too heavy for his tastes. It seemed that Andy was now taking charge of the band Brian had created. With the added complication of cocaine to fuel their "star" egos fights within the band became spectacular, things were turning sour within the Sweet. Brian was apt to declare that he would leave the band to get into acting and record a solo album but in 1975 he did no such thing. Andy had already tried for some success away from the band with his own group called Angel. He and Mick had written and produced two singles for them. Neither of the records became hits though 'Good Time Fanny' certainly would have been a smash had it been recorded by Sweet. Andy deemed the number too commercial for Sweet, an idea that Chinn and Chapman would have found baffling! After Angel were dropped Andy tried for a solo hit with the song Lady starlight, this was released a few weeks after 'Action'. It is a perfectly nice song but despite some airplay and TV appearances Andy's hopes of solo fame were dashed. Suddenly the business of writing hit songs was not looking as easy as Chinn and Chapman had made it seem.

# Strung Up

**Shortly** after the release of 'Action', Sweet released a luxurious double album titled Strung Up. The art work for the cover is the very best of Sweet's career, the illustration by Joe Petagno, a cartoon of the four members in close up, pulling the strings that control their own puppet likenesses is truly outstanding. The message conveyed by these images was that "we are our own puppet masters now"

One of the discs contains live recordings from a concert at London's Rainbow theatre, the other a selection of recent tracks already available plus what would today be termed a "bonus" track called 'I Wanna Be Committed'. This would have been the next Sweet single written by Chinn and Chapman. Listening to the song it is obvious that at this point in time both Sweet and Chinn and Chapman had manoeuvred themselves into a corner. 'I Wanna Be Committed' was too heavy by far especially at the end, the American's faded the song early when it was released there.

Strung Up is a pointless exercise, it's cover blurb, written by Radio DJ Tony Prince exclaims that having undone the strings "Andy, Steve, Mick and Brian have begun to prove that they make bloody good puppeteers! "

This was a remark in reference to the LPs title, itself a statement of independence from the tyranny and multi platinum status of life under Chinn and Chapman. They were free, free to make their own kind of music, their own kind of hits; their destiny was now in their own hands. That was the sentiment behind the album but in truth, this stylish and lush looking product contained nothing new except a cancelled Chinn and Chapman single, a single that would have probably done better than 'Action' purely on the duos reputation and selling power.

The album is indulgent to a degree that would not be tolerated by the public today, just five songs per side on the studio disc and only seven songs in total on the live one! With a total of just seventeen tracks this double LP has only five more songs on it than a standard twelve tracker. If this was Sweet's declaration of independence from Chinn and Chapman why did it contain not one but five of their songs? In truth Strung UP is a crass "hotch potch" of songs already available and a very premature slap on the back for a band about to drop off the commercial radar. Prince also asserts at the start of his piece that many have claimed that without Chinn, Chapman and Wainman writing and producing their hits Sweet would not have enjoyed the success they have had. He then goes on to say that after listening to this album the public would disagree. FIVE of the songs on the album were written by Chinn and Chapman and three of them were produced by Wainman.

Who ever decided "lets put out an album full of live versions of B sides and some old Chinn and Chapman hits, that'll convince the public of Sweets autonomy as writers" should have been fired!

The album failed to spend a day on the UK chart and only contributed to the slide going on elsewhere. Determined to leave all traces of their pop past behind them Brian, Andy, Steve and Mick also left a huge part of their audience too.

# Aint No Body Gonna Take My Place?

**The** opening lines of the Sweet's third try at a hit single were ironic to say the least. In Germany their single 'Lies In Your Eyes' went to number five, out performing 'Bohemian Rhapsody' which peaked there at number seven. They were consistently out running Queen who would forever more be seen as a band that copied Sweet.

Alas the rest of the world did not share the Germans point of view.

On January 24th 1976 all looked well for Sweet and their new offering, which entered the UK, top 50 at a respectable number 39. 'Action' had taken its first breath at number 38 so it looked as though it was business as usual. Noel Edmunds played the song each morning on the prestigious breakfast show on Radio one. Not content with only playing the single he also had a lot of fun by returning again and again to the falsetto ending note that, as a gimmick, ran all the way onto the ejector track of the record. At 15-minute intervals he would exclaim, "They're still at it" while playing the songs final note in the background.

Despite all this attention seven days after the release of 'Lies In Your Eyes' the Sweet finally came undone.

'Alexander Graham Bell' had stalled at 33 five years earlier but it had been a deliberately less commercial single. 'Turn It Down' had stalled at 41 in late 74 but it was an obvious dud and an inappropriate song to release for a hit. For all its faults, 'Lies In Your Eyes' was a fair effort, easy on the ear, catchy and accepted readily by radio stations for prime time airplay. 'Lies In Your Eyes' climbed just four places to number 35 where it stalled, slumped back to number 39 and sank into obscurity.

For Sweet breaking away from Chinn and Chapman had been to a catastrophic failure in commercial terms and the humiliation hit them hard.

To make matters worse Chinn and Chapman had continued to dominate the charts worldwide, especially with their newest acquisition Smokie.

Despite the huge shift in pop music with the coming of Punk Rock and American disco music Chinn and Chapman were holding their own. In the twelve months since Sweet had ditched Batman and Robin, their one time mentors had charted records with Suzi Quattro, Arrows, MUD and Smokie. The thorn in Sweet's side now became Chinichaps's continued success, success that only served to highlight Sweet's song writing deficiencies. Times may have changed but Mike and Nicky could still pull it off.

The biggest problem with 'Lies In Your Eyes' was that it bore an uncanny likeness to 'Satisfaction' by the Rolling Stones. The riff repeats, are very similar.

Chinn and Chapman would frequently borrow from known genres such as Country, Blues or Rock, even Latin, (MUD's first two hits were tango's) what they rarely did was borrow directly from other peoples material.

As sweet slid off the radar in the UK people had begun to notice how changed Brian's appearance had become. Three years earlier while performing 'Blockbuster' on TV he had looked beautiful, a perfect pop icon, the platinum blond pageboy, pretty, slender and slightly androgynous. In January '73 he was without doubt the prettiest star; by January '76 he was looking his age, his real age and not the one he had fibbed about for so long. Anyone wishing the public to believe they are five years younger than they actually are has a job on their hands to stay looking five years younger too. Brian had gained weight and his face was becoming puffy, he had also stopped bleaching his hair which took the edge off his look when on camera. On the home front he and Marilyn were expecting their second child though this time the press showed little interest. Though the band was very busy touring, the demand for them to appear on TV to promote singles was far less. On days when he had nothing to do work wise Brian would often start the day with a drink at the pub, occasionally he would have one or two before he left the house. Mick drank heavily too and Steve Priest has admitted to wild binges during his rock star heyday but it seems Brian was developing quite a problem. Brian was a deeply insecure person who had used fame as a way of proving to the world that he was some one. This had worked temporarily during the five years of glory though it had ultimately been a hollow victory. The approval of thousands is no substitute for true self-esteem. Within the band he and Andy were at loggerheads most of the time Brian arriving at recording studios simply to lay down his vocals. Andy was as temperamental as a lead guitarist could be and this irked both Brian and Steve. Steve was laid back to the point of falling over and it was his dry sense of humour that often stopped the fights getting out of hand. On more than one occasion Andy walked off stage at gigs because he couldn't get the right sound form his guitar amp. After one particular prima donna episode Mick refused to talk to Andy for over a week, making the atmosphere on a tour of Japan intolerable.

'Lies In Your Eyes' flopped in the USA terminating a short run of five hits and ending the possibility of the band earning the really big bucks that they had all aspired to. Andy's view with regard Brian's displeasure with the newer material was simple, if you don't like it either get out or write something better, Brian didn't do the former and couldn't do the latter.

# Give us a drink...
# We're Sloshed Angels

Trying as hard as they were, Sweet missed a subtle point about adults and adult music, there needs to be emotion, some how, some where there needs to be an element of romance. Adults, students in particular are at a very romantic stage in life. Sweet were no longer aiming at the current 12 or 13 year olds of the day, they were seeking to chase their original followers, kids who were now heading off to college or work. While it would have been inappropriate for the band to begin singing romantic slush, they were not attending to affairs of the heart at all. The Sweet was a pop group, this was not negotiable, history had seen to that. The only way to escape being a pop group would be to become more successful as a heavy rock band than they had ever been in commercial pop. After a dozen Chinnichap hits and their own 'Fox On The Run' it was unlikely that Sweet or any other band could repeat that kind of success in the heavy Rock genre. No band to date has ever reinvented itself in such a way and at such a late stage in a career. 'Lost Angels' was Sweet's first total "flop" in the UK. Released in July 1976 'Lost Angels' sounded exactly like "Fallen Angel" (11); which had just been a hit for Frankie Valli. Both records were released only weeks apart so it is doubtful that Sweet copied the ex Four Seasons vocalist's number. More likely it was Andy's falsetto tendencies reacting in the exact same way to the phrasing of the word Angel-*"Lost Ain-jels gonna take control"-"Fallen Ain-jel gotta feeling in your soul"*. Valli's popularity was soaring at the time after he had carved a niche in the domain of Disco. Apart from the chorus similarity, the drum work had a similar feel to it too, which again is probably due to a natural conclusion musically rather than plagiarism. Either way 'Lost Angels' bombed everywhere except Germany where once again Sweet were up against Queen and won! Queens's follow up to 'Bohemian Rhapsody' reached number fourteen while 'Lost Angels' ran out of steam at number thirteen. This was all rather odd for Brian and Sweet who were now one of the most successful musical acts of all time on German soil. In Germany they had achieved what they set out to do, they were Rock music's ultimate recording act, transcending all styles and fashions over a six-year period and enjoying sixteen consecutive top twenty hits. Indeed almost all their records had been top ten. Having performed on TV in the afternoon they would be escorted to the airport amid tight security ushered through the VIP lounge and onto a plane bound for the UK. Once off the plane at Heathrow they were four forgotten failed stars, able to walk about unnoticed. Brian's ego in particular was not pleased with this disparity. He was thirty-one and had certainly missed his chance to jump ship while his currency was still high. In Germany Sweet could fill a stadium, in Britain they were being offered fifteen grand a week to do cabaret shows with the proviso that they do their early Chinnichap hits. They refused all such offers; instead through out 1976 they toured the world pushing their earnings for 1975/76 through the roof. This looked great in the moment but there was no new product on the way. There had been an album titled Give Us A Wink, ignored in the UK unsurprisingly it did well in Scandinavia and was a top ten hit in Germany.

One of the reasons for the albums failure to catch on in the UK was the amount of heavy rock material on it. They were trying too hard to be as loud as Deep Purple while still trying to enjoy hit singles. The outcome was failure in both areas. Several of the songs on the album Give Us A Wink were great tunes that might have been hit singles except for the amount of guitar work on them. 'The 4th Of July' is a great song, better by far than any single released that year but no one was around to temper the egos of four seasoned rock stars in the studio.

Despite not working with Chinn and Chapman for some time Sweet's records still had the words made under licence for Chinnibridge Ltd printed on the label. They may have been writing and producing their own material for the past two years but they were still partly owned by Chinn, Chapman and Phil Wainman, all of who were part of the production company that owned Sweet's products. This meant that, though they now sold relatively few copies, the Sweet's recordings still produced an income stream for Nicky, Mike and Phil. As 1976 came to an end Sweet really began to wind down, they returned home to Chorleywood and Gerrards Cross to celebrate Christmas as "has beens" in their home land. Phil Wainman had done well after his sacking, producing two hits for MUD in 1975, the classic 'Show Me You're A Woman', which he co wrote and two number ones for the Bay City Rollers by way of the songs 'Bye Bye Baby' and 'Give A Little Love', the latter was written by him too. Chinn and Chapman ended the year with four UK hits under their belts. The members of Sweet drank and snorted their way through the humiliation of failure. They knew that unless they could come up with some sizable hit singles for the US and the UK they were doomed. They each had big houses, big cars and big spending habits. Brian had his boat, his horses, his five bedroom mansion house and his family. Andy now had a wife and son, Steve was experiencing marital problems and for all of them this was the last year on a rock star income. Of all of the band members Mick was the best with money. His excesses were contained to some degree and he was not self destructive by nature. Mick had acquired a large house in Chorleywood, Hertfordshire and had married his Sweet heart, Pauline.

Of all the members of Sweet only Brian truly began to show the seeds of destruction. As 1977 began, his star had faded badly in all territories except Germany and he hated not being a star. It is the bane of all pop acts that when failure comes it is very public and impossible to hide. Increasingly Brian would become bitter when drunk, he also started 1977 with no tour dates what so ever to keep him busy. It was too cold to sail or ride but not to cold to drink and this he did, as early as ten in the morning. As Marilyn prepared to give birth to baby Michele, Brian began living in his own little world. A world where once drunk he would re-live his glory days watching videos of himself and Sweet.

He had taken very little part in the making of the bands soon to be released album, showing up just in time to be taught his lyrics and the melodies for the vocals. Truth be known he had lost faith in Sweet and wanted to leave but the timing was now all wrong, they were down and interest in anything he might do as a solo act would be meagre indeed.

Smokie were now celebrating after having had seven big hits, hits that were far more like the kind of thing Brian wanted to sing. Brian could only watch from the sidelines while Chris Norman and his band climbed the charts again and again with Chinnichap songs such as 'Living Next Door to Alice' or 'Mexican Girl'.

Brian was increasingly trapped by his alcohol dependency and his lack of creative talent. He was a singer and performer, not a songwriter or producer. When drunk he would fantasise about reviving his career and having solo hits but he simply didn't possess the gifts that were required on his own, he needed Chinn and Chapman but they wouldn't budge. It is not clear if he ever asked them to write for him but they had made it clear that Sweet would never record another Chinn/Chapman song again.

**Left**: After Sweet Brian released three solo singles
**Above**: Heavy Smoking and drinking helped damage Brian's voice beyond repair Photo (Dick Barnatt) 1979

# Strictly Off The Record

**Sweet** began 1977 with the release of a single called the "Fever Of Love', the Dutch and the Germans loved it, in fact it took Sweet back into the top ten there for the first time in over a year.

In the UK they couldn't get arrested, in some ways they had brought this upon themselves. With punk rock dominating the airwaves, the early seventies pop and rock acts were looking either corny or in some cases pretentious. Where once Slade and Gary Glitter had exercised total domination over the British charts they were now relying on live shows to keep in touch with their audience. With his chart career behind him Marc Bolan had found a place on TV with his show Marc. The Sweet on the other hand had not played a note in a British concert hall since 1974. In their heyday their absence was considered aloof and only served to increase their godlike status, now the crash had come it only served to bury them. Without hits, concerts or any decent PR strategy they had become totally forgotten.

None of the oldies were having it easy, the punks and New wave acts had a totally different energy to the likes of Sweet, Slade or even Queen. One big difference that was emerging was the end of Rock music as part of the show business mainstream culture. Gone were the days when Cilla Black and Marc Bolan would share a stage on her TV show, or Lulu would record with David Bowie. The late seventies had returned to a counter culture in music rather than having a good laugh and wearing some make up. Brian and Co. were rather too old to jump on board the punk bandwagon and Andy's guitar work far too complicated for the new wave. The coming year would be a challenge for even the mighty Queen as the problem of where to fit in-between punk and disco overtook almost all other considerations.

Though neither The Sex Pistols nor The Stranglers had had much chart impact by February 77 the contrast in their music and Sweet's couldn't have been more glaring.

At the end of March the band released its final RCA studio album, Off the record. It contained some good songs, especially a track called 'Live For Today' which was a nod toward punk rock and could have made a good single had it been produced in a more commercial way. For the first time in years the band had recorded a ballad by way of the song 'Laura Lee'. Brian's performance on this song is one of his best but the simplicity of the number is spoiled by the amount of guitar work toward the end. The album was written in the studio for the most part, which was not particularly inspiring though it was highly expensive.

RCA records, having seen the band's sales drop by seventy percent in two years decided not to renew Sweet's contract. Both sides were obliged to supply and release one more single and a compilation album by the end of the year.

As March gave way to April it became clear that there would be no Sweet tour of any kind in 1977. They were in their second year without a hit in many territories and all four agreed that they did not want to work the cabaret type venues that were the refuge for many an ex chart act of the day.

Queen misjudged the market too, following the huge 'Somebody To Love', a huge number two record with 'Tie Your Mother Down' that stalled at a lowly number thirty-four at the start of 1977.

If these acts were to survive it would take every ounce of cunning and talent they had to carve a new niche for themselves in the post Glam era.

Chinnibridge Ltd was now making very little money, however what little it did make for Chinn, Chapman and Wainman was for no effort what so ever.

Wainman was now working with a new band called XTC. Chinn and Chapman managed to supply Suzi Quattro with a hit called 'Tear Me Apart' and also maintain the impetus with Smokie who enjoyed three more hits in 1977.

While with Chinnichap Sweet enjoyed success that came with the widest of audiences and thus when they lost this broad appeal there was no hiding the fact.

At this point in time there was no one around to take away the excesses that frequently trip up musicians who undertake self-production. There seems to be more egos on Off The Record than editing.

In July the band offered 'Stairway To The Stars' as its final RCA single, the British music press labelled it "tripe" and "money for old rope" The latter comment being painfully true. The song is a lack lustre re write of 'Alright Now' by the band Free and an amalgamation of all Sweet's recent failures. To all concerned, media, fans and critics it seemed as though Sweet were a totally spent force by mid 77.

Counting their blessings the four bruised egos boarded a plane bound for Munich to promote their song to the faithful. In Germany their Stairway climbed to number fifteen.

Queen released an EP at the same time as 'Stairway To The Stars', simply called Queens first EP it managed to peak at Number 17.

A slowly dying era came to an abrupt end with the shocking news that Marc Bolan, epitome of all things seventies and glam rock was dead. While travelling home in the early hours with girlfriend Gloria Jones, their Mini had run off the road and into a tree, he died instantly. The Sex Pistols were number one with God Save the Queen.

Sweet parted company with RCA records at the end of 1977. The final release was a disastrous compilation titled Sweet's Golden Greats. While it was true that the band were very out of fashion in late '77 and had totally neglected their UK fans for years, the LP failed catastrophically for two reasons.

The cover of the Album is a contemporary late 70s design using an up to date photo of the band looking pensive and a little past their glam rock gorgeousness. Mick looks happy in a close up, if a little unstylish while Steve looks radiant and mischievous but its not a good cover for a look back at earlier glories. Dodgy cover art aside, it is the selections and omissions on the disc that caused its complete failure in the UK. Desperate to be taken more seriously than they had been at home, Sweet and the powers that be saw fit to release a greatest hits LP with all the early hits missing.

What should have been a TV advertised 20 track banquet of bubblegum, Glam Rock and even a few heavy rock anthems, wrapped in a cover of nostalgic photos, was in fact a rather dull LP with a few old hits and a couple of flops.

There are no rock stars that handle failure well but the wise will see it as part of the business they are in. The art of learning from failure is not to repeat it, yet Sweet had repeated it on their singles in ever decreasing circles.

Back in Gerrards Cross even Brian realised that something had to be done about his drinking. Instead of drinking on a daily basis he decided there would be times when he would be dry. The result was periods of irritable misery followed by huge uncontrollable binging.

Marilyn kept the children out of his way when he was on a binge but despite her best efforts her pleas for him to seek help were at best ignored and at times simply laughed at.

The band had seen less and less of each other as 1977 went on but that was about to change. Ed Leffler and David Walker had secured a deal with Polydor records. Polydor was very big in Germany, the only market Sweet was still known in. If things were kept on a modest scale in the studio and on tour they could still make some good money.

While all of the members of the band have admitted to living the Rock star life style by the end of the seventies and getting up to some crazy things, three of them were able to knuckle under when duty called. Brian was not one of them. As a singer he had to endure long hours waiting for his turn to do his vocals. That is the price he had to pay for all the attention. Many singers are not present for a large part of the process of making records. Brian now had little or no promotion work to keep him out of trouble and unlike the rest of the band he was apt to go off the deep end when under the influence.

As the time rolled round for the band to start recording their make or break Polydor debut, Andy's opinion of Brian was at rock bottom.

Andy was a home bird; happy to be immersed in the music he was creating. His ego required artistic and critical recognition, Brian's adoration and stardom via the media and his audience.

Brian didn't rate Andy's efforts at supplying him with hits, Andy was spitting mad with Brian's unreliability, especially his habit of missing rehearsals and recording sessions. Neither had the demands of stardom to divert attention from their animosity, indeed it was the pressure of failure that would push them into the confines of a studio for the last time.

# Who's The King of the Castle?

**After** the experience of writing "on the hoof" in the studio during the making of Off The Record Sweet were determined not to repeat the experience for their next album. What they needed was inspiration and a new sound, although slightly begrudgingly, this was instigated by Andy. He and Mick wanted with all their hearts to become known as heavy metal band but the slump in sales called for a radical re think. At the end of August all four of them de camped to Clearwell Castle in the West of England. Situated in the Forest of Dean, it was no coincidence that Sweet chose this gothic pile as venue for their make or break moment. Five years earlier Deep Purple had finished their famous Burn album there and given a press conference on the lawn. Though they were following in Purples foot steps quite literally now, Sweet were going it alone on the music front.

The drive took a little over an hour and a half from London to the Castle gates but the four decided to stay at the place so as to "soak up the atmosphere" Brian had been miss behaving lately and had managed to upset all of the band, as this was the case he decided to keep his distance. In a three story gothic castle this was not too difficult, he simply stayed in his own wing. By now none of the band were in great shape, in his autobiography "Ready Steve" Sweet's bass player readily admits that they were all heavily into alcohol and stimulants such as cocaine, they had even put JJ Cale's famous song about the drug into their live set at the end of their last tour.

During that tour the group had headlined at the Santa Monica Civic Auditorium to a massive and enthusiastic crowd. On the final night they were joined on stage by Ritchie Blackmore of Deep Purple, at that moment all seemed to be as it should be for Brian Connolly and Sweet. Alas it was built on the foundations of earlier hits and tails were now firmly between legs at Clearwell castle.

In spite of their present precarious position the band were far too used to indulgence to simply "get on with it". They spent the first two days just wandering around the castle, which had many treasures and curiosities to look at.

They played cricket in the afternoon and stayed up most of the night after visiting the local pub. Cases of wine were delivered to the castle in the foolish belief that they may oil the works and get the band moving. At last work began in earnest; they were working with other musicians for the first time in years. This was a good thing that would bring fresh life and new colours to the bands music, however they were far too self important by now to let the presence of others temper their eccentricities, they were after all, the Sweet.

Brian's behaviour became very unpredictable and his voice suffered terribly from the relentless punishment of chain smoking and daylong boozing sessions. At the end of the first week he went home for a break! On his return he became fixated with a plan to jump from a roof and survive. Generally the story told describes him jumping from a roof that was fifty feet high, landing on a mobile recording studio and walking into the castle declaring, "I fucking told you I could do it". While much of the story could be true the fifty foot part is certainly fiction as that would have placed him several floors higher than the castle, not to mention being physically impossible.

The Connolly marriage was now almost a sham, despite her love for Brian Marilyn had learned to cut herself off from her erring husband. She had recently given birth to daughter Michele but her husband, far from being a doting father was unfaithful, unpredictable, unstable and drunk. He had frequently had the shakes in his younger days after heavy nights boozing. Now it became clear that his day had to begin with a drink just to help him function.

As is almost always the case when addiction takes over, Brian was in total denial of his predicament. At long last the Sweet was making the kind of music he had longed to sing yet his actions were ruining his big chance of renewed success.

At home Marilyn was becoming more and more isolated spending her days looking after two young children. Seventy miles away Brian continued to enjoy the company of groupies who were readily available at the castle.

It wasn't all bad vibes and quick tempers, on a few occasions when the sun shone and the crew took a break they were entertained by a band that had truly been around the block and had plenty of stories to regale. There were of course the run-ins with the law. One because of milk bottles in

Cricklewood, another because of their "lewd" stage act in Belgium both of those resulted in a spell in the cells for Brian and Steve. Another narrow escape had been during the photo shoot for Sweet's biggest hits. The band were in their 'Wig Wam Bam' outfits sitting in front of a kids plastic wig wam in Hyde Park when a policeman arrived, apparently a member of the public had thought that Andy was showing a little too much thigh and it was the "Copper's" unenviable duty to check that underwear was being worn!

In 1974 Brian had worn his famous Tiger emblem on T shirts and the like, as a final publicity stunt for Tony Barrow's enterprises Brian posed for Bravo magazine with a real live tiger cub in his arms. This was a strange thing to ask Brian to do as it was MUD who were number one with 'Tiger Feet', perhaps Les Grey simply didn't like the idea. Up for anything, Brian lifted the cub into his arms, however after a few minutes the animal got the jitters and tore most of the sleeve off of Brian's leather jacket. They had come a long way all right but not without paying the price of fame in full.

With their previous history it was inevitable that Brian and Andy would soon clash and when they did it was primarily over the quality of Brian's vocals. He was thirty-three years old and neither his looks nor his voice could with stand the punishment he forced upon them.

Vocally he was constantly hoarse and it took many takes before he could deliver an acceptable performance. Luckily for him it had become common to join many different slices of vocal together to create a single performance. Still, tugging away on forty Benson and Hedges a day it was a miracle he could sing at all.

That seemed to be the biggest issue at Clearwell as the summer ended but there was another problem equally pressing.

As time went on and the style of the new album began to emerge it became clear that this was not a heavy rock platter about to be served. Sweet had returned to what they had always done so well, ultra melodic pop. It was much more mature with occasional overtones of Lead Zeppelin and the like but power chording and distortion were not part of the recipe being prepared at the castle.

As this was the case they may at last have a chance of scoring a hit single but after two years in the wilderness it would have to be something special. Try as he may Andy was just not coming up with anything like an obvious hit. Confidence was in short supply too; after all, their track record beyond the German boarder was abysmal in the singles department. It had seemed that after their early experiences with session musicians the band had an aversion to any outside contributions on their records. That all changed once they arrived at Clearwell castle.

Geoff Westley would assist with musical arrangements, Gary Moberly with Keyboards and a young man named Trevor Griffin would inadvertently provide the band with its next hit single.

'Love Is Like Oxygen' started life as a piece of film score that Griffin was working on at the time. Having overheard snatches from the piece Andy Scott asked Griffin if he could use one of the themes.

Only a fool would refuse as the new album by Sweet was showing great promise. 'Love Is Like Oxygen' was one of the final tracks recorded for the album and by now Andy and Brian were no longer speaking. Brian recorded his part of the song with Mick Tucker at another studio a little later and the result surprised every one.

Crystal clear, bang on key Brian's verses sparkled and sounded completely integral to the finished product. If this didn't do the trick in the top forty nothing would.

With 1977 almost over the jury was still out as to whether Queen and Sweet would survive the onslaught of Punk Rock and Disco music.

Up till November Queens highest placing with a single that year had been number thirty-four. 'We Are The Champions' entered the UK chart gingerly gaining momentum slowly week on week. Eventually the song found its way to Number two, egged on by its B Side 'We Will Rock You' which picked up nearly as many plays as 'We Are The Champions'. With a smash hit under their belt Queen had jumped the ravine and added two of their best known tunes to a rapidly growing repertoire.

# Pride Always Comes Before a Fall

**The** shelf life of a single is dependant on several factors, not least by the state of the career of the artist. The more popular an act, the more often its recordings will feature on radio. Sweet were to have no more hits and would shortly be dealt a death blow yet 'Love Is Like Oxygen' continued to be a popular choice for radio DJs well into the 80s purely because of its originality and excellent production. Selling steadily around the globe the number sold over a million copies and earned writers Andy Scott and Trevor Griffen, Ivor Novelo awards to boot.

Just as several of the group's consecutive number two hits were better than the numbers that "pipped them to the post", 'Love Is Like Oxygen' also deserved a better placing in the charts. The reason for its slightly sluggish performance was simply down to Sweet's unpopularity in the weeks prior to the records release.

When it stumbled into the chart at a lowly number forty eight it must have seemed like deja-vu for Brian and Steve as this was where it had all began with 'Funny Funny' seven years earlier. Within a week the song had stormed the top thirty and phones began ringing once again. In all of the territories lost to Sweet, the UK had been the first to see them go and the first to see them return. With no TV appearances for the last two years the British public were literally shocked by Brian's appearance when he re appeared on Top of the pops. While 'Lies In Your Eyes' and 'Action' counted as statistical hits for sure, the last time the image of Brian Connolly had stuck in the public's mind was during the promotion of 'Fox On The Run'. The difference between that Brian and the bleary eyed puffy faced aberration of 1978 set tongues wagging.

Two weeks later the song was at number nine and the group celebrated its "first" ten years together with a splurge of articles in the music press. At last they had a way to return to the UK as a success rather than as a chicken in the basket cabaret act. With this in mind a date was added to their European tour, they were to play at the Hammersmith Odeon at the end of February. The gig sold out in days surprising everyone, it seemed that the faith full had been patiently waiting for the prodigals to return and when they finally did all wanted front row seats.

On the evening of the show all went like clockwork with wives, families and several members of rock royalty in attendance. Even Nicky Chinn went back stage to congratulate the Sweet as it roared back into life. Rather telling is the fact that following the after show party in the theatre, Andy, Steve and Mick went along to a gathering to celebrate together while Brian went alone to another event.

For the first time in years the members of Sweet were being regarded properly in the UK, no longer a bunch of Brits big in Germany, they were a bunch of Brits big in Britain!

# Batman and Robin....
## Utterly unstoppable!

**Just** as Brian and the band began to feel they had at last out paced their reputation as a failed ex Chinnichap act, Suzi Quattro enjoyed a huge hit with 'If you cant give me love', peaking at number four it did considerably better than Sweet's single and it was written by Chinn and Chapman. If this wasn't bad enough the Sweet took off for America on tour without releasing a follow up to their comeback hit. Their position in the recording industry was far from secure and the first rule of releasing hit singles is issue a follow up immediately.

The tour became plagued with problems, many to do with Brian, twice he pitched up on stage wasted after spending the day with groupies, so wasted that his performance was atrocious. One of these occasions was in Birmingham, Alabama.

In the US the band was signed to Capitol records, the company had recently gotten over a bad case of the jitters with regard Sweet, whose sales had collapsed in late 76. Suddenly they had an album and single in the charts and it looked very likely that several hits could be lifted from the new disc. As this was the case Ed Leffler took Capitol's top brass along to see the revived Sweet in action. With monumental bad timing, Brian chose this occasion to become so addled that the show had to be abandoned after only a few songs, Brian wandering about the stage at one point holding a conversation with a speaker!

The single made the US top ten, the album entered the US top forty and the bands reputation with its US distributors hit the floor. The main problem for Brian in Alabama was that it was a "Dry state". Without alcohol, which he could moderate with a small degree of success, he resorted to pills (downers); he simply could not recover from them in time for the show. It is unlikely by this stage of his addiction that he could have performed without either first being de-toxed or continuing to drink in order to help him function. Without either option, he had 'tranquilised' himself into oblivion and then attempted to sing 'Ballroom Blitz'.

The four returned home, one of them determined that "enough was enough".

The album Level Headed contained many gems, not least the songs 'Silver Bird' and Lady Of The Lake'. 'Silver Bird' had all the "bang for your buck" that 'Fox On The Run' had delivered three years earlier but it also took the theme in to more subtle territory. The Sweet was by now a very old band indeed, they had publicly celebrated the tenth anniversary in March and the next release had the potential to become Sweet's seventeenth UK chart hit.

Whether they liked it or not, the public saw Sweet as one of the old groups, as something almost from the sixties. Luckily they were enjoying a chart hit and so despite being old they were still current to some degree. Had 'Silver Bird' been issued in May 1978 it would without doubt have become a very big hit for Sweet. It had a good strong narrative for

Brian to sing, a strong high pitch chorus and as many catchy hooks as a Chinnichap number. May gave way to June, June to July and in August it was announced that the band were to begin recording a new album, once again at the castle.

No follow up was ever issued to 'Love Is Like Oxygen' in the UK or any other territory other than Germany. As time passed the public began to mistakenly attribute the song to 10cc or ELO. This was in part because the Sweet disappeared so quickly after its release and thus it was not fully associated with the band. In Germany the pressure to release another record was irresistible so the band went with the track 'California Nights'. This was a catastrophic mistake as it was one of the weaker songs on the album as far as singles potential. Sung by Steve Priest, the record stumbled its way to number twenty three in Germany, Sweet looking entirely wrong with their star Brian standing to one side strumming a guitar.

The decision to release the record only in Germany amply demonstrates the lack of confidence Polydor records had in the tune at the time.

As August arrived in 1978 Sweet were once more becoming forgotten, one hit single in January and a concert in February would not be enough activity to keep them in the British public eye.

In Mid August Nicky Chinn and Mike Chapman's newest project Racy flew into the chart with the song, 'Lay Your Love On Me', which peaked at number three. Suzi Quattro was back in the top fifty with 'The Race Is On'. Even though they were now the peddlers of pure corn the public still loved Chinn and Chapman's songs.

It is not possible to know exactly who decided that no track using Brian would be used as a single from the bands comeback LP, but the decision proved fatal.

A likely scenario would be that it was felt too risky to place Brian centre stage for the promotion of a new record; he had been off the rails for months and could not always be relied on. Andy had never been a fan of his lead singer and for Brian's part the feeling was mutual. It is likely that Scott wanted to see if they could get along without the troublesome singer. He had been a driving force in the split from Chinn and Chapman. 'California Nights' sent Steve Priest's profile sky high in Germany, for a few short weeks he became the star of the Sweet, until it was obvious that the song was stalling in the lower twenties.

Standing miming with a guitar (he neither played nor sang on the song) Brian Connolly performed for the last time with his beloved Sweet.

**Below**: left, a posthumous collection featuring Brian's un-finished works
**Below**: right, Let's GO, Brian's penultimate recordings from 1996

**Above:** left, The US Desolation Boulevard is an amalgam of two albums
**Above;** Right; Brian Connolly sings on only one of the nine tracks of this 'exploitation' disc, the other singer is 60s 'wanna- be' Brian Connell.

# Three Piece Sweet, Going Cheap

In February 1979 the music press announced that the new Sweet single 'Call Me' would be released shortly, the accompanying pictures showed just three members of Sweet, Brian was gone.

The official line was that he had left the band to pursue solo projects and an album would follow shortly. The story down the years has always centred on the making of the album Cut Above The Rest. Brian's only involvement was to lay down his vocal tracks. Once again this was done in isolation because he and Andy were not on speaking terms. Brian and Mick went alone to a studio on several occasions in November 78 and after one of these sessions Steve and Andy followed on after to take a listen to the results.

Unable to quit smoking and still drinking heavily Brian's work was not up to standard. There are a few tracks remaining from these sessions and while they may not be 'award winning stuff' there is little evidence of a disaster either. Had the band been friends, particularly Scott and Connolly, allowances could have been made for the aging singers shortcomings. Instead Andy became resolute, he wanted Brian gone. Brian's voice was wiped, some of the numbers rewritten and the destruct button firmly pressed, whether they knew it or not.

'Call Me' was a fair effort, written entirely by Andy, its chorus is a very fitting follow up to 'Love Is Like Oxygen', however that record had appeared thirteen months earlier, an eternity in the pop world. The verses of the song are clumsy and the extended version terribly dated even for the day. In 1979 a wry reference to petroleum jelly was neither clever nor funny.

In the UK 'Call Me' was top of the play list and looked set to do something but after a week of heavy play on radio one it failed to make even the newly extended top 75 chart. In Germany the song staggered to number twenty-nine, it was Sweet's final hit there, the groups twenty first since 1971. There remains some TV footage of the three performing 'Call Me'. It looks entirely unconvincing, as if they do not believe in the material they are singing, material written by them. Steve Priest spends more time looking at Andy than he does at the camera thus Brian's absence is felt all the more, the blonde one would have been centre stage singing direct to camera with great conviction. His delivery may have become a little dated but he knew what the lead singer's job was.

The single's job was to act as a springboard for the new album, it failed and without a hit the album stiffed too. With no recent hits and no lead singer Sweet's viability as a live act evaporated, by April 79 even offers from Cabaret style venues were gone. MUD, Slade, Gary Glitter, all the oldies had seen their recording careers slide but they had all toured the halls regularly, they were also still intact. The fans knew who they were and where to find them. Sweet had played live in the UK just once in five years, had only one hit in the last three and now had lost the man who sang 'Blockbuster'; they were simply three musicians with a rather large recording contract.

Brian festered in Gerrards Cross, to some degree a hollow victory had been won, he was after all indispensable, as far as the public were concerned Brian Connolly was The Sweet.

Polydor records were dismayed, how had it all gone so terribly wrong? Similarly Ed Leffler and David walker now found that they were managing thin air.

A deal was hatched with Polydor to give Brian two singles and the possibility of an album, Sweet were still signed for another year to the company and records would occasionally be released with the letters S W E E T on the label but in truth the last Sweet record to hit the shops was 'Call Me', it at least sounded like a Sweet record minus Brian Connolly. By July Steve had lost all interest in the band and realised that the game was up, he was persuaded to stay by way of the song; 'Big Apple Waltz'. He had written it as a love ballad to his new wife and so was delighted when it became the next single. Nice song though it is, it was a lousy choice for a single and has the dubious honour of being the first Sweet record to flop in every corner of the world, even the Germans preferred not to take a partner for this particular waltz.

There was much bitterness at this point as all four of the players saw their fame fortune and reputations go down the drain. For three of them it had been like surviving in a very bitter marriage breakdown, a marriage to an unstable alcoholic, promising time and time again to change but in reality sinking further into the abyss. Slightly worse than a marriage break up, Brian's demise would take them all down professionally too, no more hits, stadium tours, TV appearances or royalties.

Brian could be obnoxious when drunk, it is a common symptom in the disease of Alcoholism he had long since used up any sympathy felt for him by Steve and Andy. Only Mick, his original founding member had argued for a Sweet with Connolly still on board but eventually Brian had been fired, fired from his own creation.

Somehow a cocaine habit would have seemed more in keeping with the excesses of a 70s rock star, simple alcoholism really didn't add glamour to the destruction of Sweet's golden boy, it had all become rather sad. With Sweet's career destroyed it was time to see just exactly what Brian would come up with in relation to the "solo projects" mentioned in the press released of early 1979.

# 'Don't You Know A Lady'

**Sweet's** first post Brian single had been 'Call Me', it is no coincidence that the flip side of Brian's first effort post Sweet was called 'Phone You'. On listening to the lyric it becomes quite obvious that it was a message to his one-time colleagues. It is a rather dreadful song, poorly produced and sung wearily, Brian sounding possibly a little worse for the weather.

The A side of his first solo disc is another matter altogether, 'Don't You Know A Lady' is a joyous pop number, a little dated in its style but perfectly executed. It was written by Roger Greenaway and Mike Leander, the former had written 'All You Ever Get From Me' for Sweet back in 1970, Leander was Gary Glitter's writing partner and producer. As a pop song it is better than Sweet's 'Call Me' which lacked "lift" on the chorus, Brian's offering was chorus strong, very memorable and could have been a modest hit had he possessed the almighty energy and vigour that such a resurrection would need. The song had one major fault; the middle section was far too long, a rule of thumb for solo recordings by vocalists is never to have any long instrumental work. What Brian was supposed to be doing during the full minute long break in the song will forever remain a mystery; he was not a keen dancer!

Brian Connolly was very old for the pop world, it was September 1979 and in the UK his star had long since faded, nineteen months had passed since 'Love Is Like Oxygen' had put him back on British television. Prior to that there had been a break of 17 months, The class of 1979 didn't really know who he or Sweet were and at thirty four Brian was now old enough to be the father of the twelve and thirteen year olds who were the bulk of singles buyers. The single was ignored in the UK and was a modest success in Germany.

Brian had the right idea with 'Don't You Know A Lady', it was nostalgic, it had a touch of 'Little Willy' about it, it was easy to sing and dance to and so may have reached out to his former audience now in their late teens and early twenties. To do this would have meant a tour, a club tour, a cabaret type event, plus lots of radio and other PR commitments. Though he certainly wasn't a keen dancer it would have been spectacular had he promoted the single with a bevy of young "ladies" who perhaps would have danced around him while he sang it in a white suit etc. Pure showbiz maybe but he was no longer the front man of a band, he was going for all out pop stardom and 'Don't You Know A Lady' was after all a disco record. After eleven years of recordings he was looked upon as 'old hat'. Chinn and Chapman's songs were by now the oldest hat of all, yet Racy were at number two in the chart with the classic 'Some Girls'. Suzi Quattro also scored two hits in 1979, both written again by Chinn and Chapman. Phil Wainman also continued to be successful, his biggest hit of 1979 being 'I Don't Like Mondays', which he produced for the Boomtown Rats.

An aged pop star that was universally liked and respected may have swung it, perhaps scoring a top thirty hit, thus acquiring a few precious weeks of chart life to hang a solo career on. Sadly at this point Brian was the drink sodden, mistrusted, ex lead singer of a dilapidated Glam Rock group. Good will would have been essential and there was none to be had.

# Take away the music

**Brian's** follow up to 'Don't You Know A Lady' arrived in April 1980; he was now thirty-five years of age and abusing himself terribly.
His output was so meagre that Polydor records were prepared to release the single in Germany only. The song is a country type of number that was not produced in a way that would ever have appealed to the record buying public of the time.

There is little evidence to suggest that it was ever promoted in Germany beyond a few radio plays at the time of release. The B-side 'Alabama Man' is poorly produced and sung by Brian once again as if he was somewhat under the weather. He had hoped for the song to become a single, believing that it had the potential for chart success. Sadly this demonstrates how wide of the mark his opinion was with regard the pop market of the time. The charts were dominated by the likes of Police, Blondie and Michael Jackson and Brian's 'Alabama Man' fitted nowhere into that spectrum. The ultra pop market had given itself over to Disco with acts like Village People and ABBA dominating the dance floors of Northern Europe. Where as 'Don't You Know A Lady' had pitched in with the latter market as a contender, Brian's second single stood outside the fold of recognised pop at the time. This is only a good thing to do if one has created a ground breaking new style. It is often the case that an "act" does not know the best material for its commercial survival. Doris Day initially turned down 'Que Sera Sera' believing it to be a simple nursery rhyme, (it was her biggest seller) and won best song of 1956. The Beatles originally wrote 'I Wanna Hold Your Hand' as a ballad and Mick Tucker thought that 'Tiger Feet' wouldn't sell. It is probable that Polydor records were humouring Brian in his attempt to break into Country pop, allowing just a limited release of 'Take Away The Music'. He was dropped shortly after so the burden of one particular member of the band had not been too long on the books. At this time Chinn and Chapman's new band Exile were snuggled in the top ten with their song 'I Wanna Kiss You All Over', Suzi Quattro was also enjoying a modest success with the song 'Rock Hard', her final Chinnichap hit.

More than two years had elapsed since Level Headed and the success of 'Love Is Like Oxygen', yet Brian had managed to record just two singles. The last time he had been in a studio to work on a major album had been in October 1978. During late 79 and early 80 he worked at home in Gerrards cross with his manager Mick Angus. Angus had looked after some of Sweet's tours and was a good and loyal friend of Brian's. There were days when Brian straightened himself out and knuckled soberly down to work. He had the idea for, Take Away The Music', Angus developed the theme and arranged the number. Progress was painfully slow on the creative front and the direction of Brian's career lacked focus to say the least. The sentiments in the lyric of 'Take Away The Music' say it all with regard Brian's attitude at the time.

Take away the music
Take away the good times
What have I left I don't know
Take away the booze
Take away the ladies
What have I left I don't know


Like most of his peers it would have been unlikely that Brian Connolly would have been able to have re invented himself in the 1980s as a solo star. MUD's Les Grey tried with several singles the most successful being 'Groovy Kind Of Love'. Slade's Noddy Holder had to wait till a lucky break in acting occurred during the 1990s. The pop world is littered with ex lead singers who failed to set the charts alight after jumping ship from chart busting bands. Paul Jones, arguably one of the great voices of the 1960s with Manfred man recorded some truly note worthy records during the punk era in the late 70s, all of which failed commercially. Brian's solo records would probably have failed no matter what but 'Take Away The Music' stood no chance what so ever. His biggest issue was now that his main tool for survival was severely blunted; a singer with a faltering voice has a big problem.

Though never in the same league, Brian's problems in 1980 mirrored those of the great Judy Garland. Both were singers whose voices were wearing out, both were hopelessly addicted to substances and both were smokers. More than this, they were broke, both had earned amounts of cash that the ordinary man in the street would find hard to imagine yet Garland died owing over two million in1969 and in 1980 Brian was living purely on over draught. In short, they both had to keep going no matter what. He had not written 'Love Is Like Oxygen', the only member of Sweet to profit from the final hit was Andy Scott. Andy also pocketed a few extra pennies from his modest hit 'Call Me'. Brian had not earned any real money since the tour of 1978 yet his horses needed grooming, his boat mooring and his family needed to be fed.

Had he owned up to his alcoholism and his true standing in show business he may have enjoyed some considerable success at this point. He was a "has been", no ifs no buts, his fame came from the previous decade, another era. His best shot would to have been in recording an album similar to Funny How Sweet Co Co Can Be. A platter filled with a mix of cover versions, self-written tunes and a couple of professionally crafted singles. The process had started out ok with 'Don't You Know A Lady' but then the plot had been lost. Around this time he and Mick Angus wrote a tune called 'Sunshine Days', although a little derivative of 'Sweet Caroline' by Neil Diamond, it would have done Brian proud. Like many other projects of 1980 it was never finished, it is true to say that many an Alcoholic would identify with the process of starting things and never finishing them. In the past Brian had been spoilt musically, he had been the receiver of material via Sweet and in particular Mr. Scott. Seeing no light at the end of the tunnel Polydor dropped the option of the album. It was autumn, Brian was totally unemployed and as the days grew short he slid into an abyss that he would only ever partly return from.

As 1981 began and Brian turned thirty-six he left reality behind, he was utterly consumed with bitterness about his sacking from Sweet. Work on his album stalled completely. The three-piece Sweet turned in an album and a couple of singles, all of which failed in every country they were released in. They had even played some live gigs on the university circuit but it couldn't work. They were years past the big time and to pull a ticket buying audience they required a lead singer, Brian. He was now in the grip of insanity, drinking round the clock. It was during a rare semi sober occasion that Brian went for a trip into London, while there he was spotted by Norman Dival, his one time press officer. Norman remembers; "It was in about the middle of '81. I was in the street near Oxford Circus when who should I see but Brian and Marilyn. She looked great but Brian, oh dear, he was so bloated that you would barely know who he was, no body did of course, just imagine the three of trying to stand there during the mid seventies, we would have been mobbed! I'd heard that he was on the booze but it wasn't till I saw him that I realised how ill he had become."

# *Hy*pnotised

**Within** a few months Brian was taken ill in the night, his body had filled with fluid as a result of his kidneys being under such stress from the alcohol. After being admitted to hospital his condition deteriorated rapidly, his heart stopped, he was revived it stopped again, then again. Luckily it started quickly after each intervention so the medical staff revived him over and over. In total it is said that he suffered almost a dozen cardiac arrests over a very short period. Marilyn was told he was gone, then that he had survived. When finally he was stabilised in the early hours the doctors broke the news that during the crisis his body had sustained such damage that he was unlikely to recover. His brain, nervous system and his vital organs were all damaged, most likely beyond repair. At eleven the next morning Brian awoke complaining that he was starving, he demanded a full English breakfast. This may have been a great start but little did he know that in the early hours the night before he had started a time bomb ticking, as he at last tucked into his grub that afternoon all looked well, in fact he was doomed.

Warned that another drink could kill him, Brian set about a fragile recovery from alcoholism. He was still banished from all things Sweet, though by early 82 the band had ceased to exist. Their Polydor deal had ended and Steve had moved to New York to start a new life. Andy was licking his wounds at his new flat in London's trendy Maida Vale, newly divorced much of his fortune had gone via income tax and the alimony settlement. Mick remained in his Rickmansworth mansion beside the newly opened M25 still convinced that a reunion might be possible.

There was a ground swell of support for Brian after his brush with death not least from Mick Angus who was about to end his association with Brian to pursue a career in America. He secured Brian a deal with the German record label Carrire, the song to be released was a collaborative number called 'Hypnotised'. During the recording sessions Brian struggled to hit several of the notes. The number was eventually spliced together though not altogether seamlessly. 'Hypnotised' sounds today like a typical generic heavy rock number from the early 80s, a far cry from the country career its singer had hoped to carve out for himself following his departure from Sweet. It was not a hit in any country, although it is rumoured that he performed it on German TV no film has ever surfaced of him doing so.

The B-side of the record was a self-penned number called 'Fade Away', in this song Brian describes his own downfall in a light hearted way. It s a country type of number which once again has far too much instrumental work in it for a record by a vocalist. The narrative of the song describes Brian walking along unnoticed in streets where once he would have been mobbed, this time he has gone too far, no one knows who he is anymore.

Much rested on the performance of 'Hypnotised' in the shops, it s singer was on the verge of becoming bankrupt. If the song was a hit and a tour followed perhaps his fortunes could be revived. Who could blame him for trying though 'Hypnotised' stood little chance on its own merits and Brian was now thirty-seven. He was also four years out of the charts and didn't seem to know where he was musically. 'Don't You Know A Lady', a disco single, Take away the music, a country single and now 'Hypnotised', a heavy rock number. The song sank like a brick and with it went Brian's prospects of financial recovery. Over at Polydor the decision was taken to release the remaining unreleased Sweet material in the guise of an album called Identity Crisis. The Identity Crisis album contained nine new tracks and was available in Germany only, no single was ever issued. The fourteen-year recording career of Brian and Sweet had come to an end. No major label would ever release original material by any of them again.

In June 1982 a young lady by the name of Toni Basil was at number two in the charts with the song 'Mickey', below the title were the words Chinn and Chapman. This release brought their total of UK hits to a staggering 54 in twelve years; 'Mickey' had started life as 'Vicky' and had been recorded by Racy. The partnership of Chinn and Chapman came to an end, it had been the decades most prolific by far and one of the most successful collaborations in recording history. Sweet had been the first act to release a Chinnichap hit and had enjoyed twelve consecutive top fifty records with the pair. After leaving Chinn and Chapman the Sweet had scored just two more top ten hits, while Chinn and

Chapman had delivered dozens more for The Arrows, MUD, Suzi Quattro, Smokie, Exile, Racy and Toni Basil. Chapman had also produced the award winning album Parallel lines for Blondie, including the classic single 'Heart of Glass'. From now on Nicky Chinn would concentrate on business interests and take it easy while Chapman would immediately write and produce a song for Tina Turner called 'Simply The Best', it would become another all time classic. Sweet had not touched the charts in five years, during that time they must have pondered many times on how different things might have been had they stayed with Chinnichap. It is a for drawn conclusion that had the band stuck with Chinn and Chapman it would have been the biggest singles band of the decade, all that was needed was perhaps another half dozen hits. Six or seven hit singles would not have made very much difference to the mighty Chinnichap roster but it would have placed Sweet and Brian Connolly in a very different position in 1983.

# April 1983...a personal memory

**One** evening, perhaps a Thursday I went along to a club called Baileys in Watford. Suzi Quattro was playing. I was twenty-one years old and with my friend Steve, he sadly died of alcoholism some years ago. Shortly before the show was to begin I looked over a balcony down toward the stage and there he was; my absolute idol Brian Connolly. I went wild, "it's him, oh my god it's him" I exclaimed. My friend Steve was a little older than me, a bit more worldly, he had heard things locally, he frowned when I said I was going down stairs to meet him, Steve refused to come with me. I approached Brian's table just as he got up to go somewhere. He looked at me, I looked at him, a besotted fan. Brian had so few to his name by 1983. My first words to Brian Connolly were, "it's you isn't it, it's really you "

We walked back up the stairs, he was going to Suzi's dressing room to say hello, he could barely make it up the stairs, said he had hurt his knee. He looked so old, he was pretty drunk and wore a pair of trousers that had a huge waist but were skintight. All these things I remember like it was yesterday not a quarter of a century ago.

We got to a door at the back of the place, he went inside, I knew by instinct that I shouldn't follow; it was a place for the stars, not a twenty one year old green grocer.

I rushed down to the DJ stand and told him of the special guest in the audience, he promised to play a couple of old Sweet records if he could find them. I returned to the door and waited for my idol, with perfect timing, he opened it as the siren began for 'Blockbuster'. I don't know if he had actually drunk more booze or it was just catching up with him but he was getting more unsteady by the minute. We found ourselves inside the doorway in a long passage. I said some waffle about him being my idol and loving him, he responded in a way that threw me. "I can give you one if you want but it might take me a while these days". I was gay for sure, but I'd never thought of Brian Connolly like that. I'd never even thought of him as human. To me he was something unreal. I'd adored him since I was nine years old. I recoiled slightly and he realised something was not quite right too. I asked him what he was doing now and he said, "We are touring" "Your back with them, oh my god, will you come to England?" Realising he had been rumbled he exploded into an emotional outburst all over me. "Its over, it's all fucking over, it's finished, nobody wants me anymore" With that he went to push me away but instead he slid halfway down the wall and I had to help him back up. While I was doing this a sort of cleaning lady figure walked up and declared that this was a private area and the public were not allowed. "This is Brian Connolly of the Sweet" I declared indignantly. "I don't care who he is, get him up and get him out of here or I'll call security." So I hoisted my idol up and helped him back to the stairs, by now Marilyn was looking for him and she helped him back down them. She looked at me a little embarrassed, I smiled turned away and burst into tears as my friend Steve said "I was afraid that would happen, everybody knows what he s like ". I had no idea. I had expected to find Brian as a retired millionaire pop star, looking great and ready to be gracious to a fan from the old days. I was twenty-one. What did I know? Suzi came on stage and did a fantastic show; Brian was carried out unconscious by his hands and feet about half way through. That was my first meeting with Brian Connolly.

# A Very Public Upheaval

As 1983 continued it became obvious that Brian would loose it all, the house, the boat, and the marriage. Poor Marilyn had been through the emotional ringer as few human beings could imagine. Her story was not rags to riches but Brian's roller coaster life had been hers too for almost twenty years. As he struggled at Vicmonds Carpets she struggled with him, loading the shopping into the back of his little mini van, occasionally joining him at The Swan or The Cley Pigeon for a drink with Mick. Then it had happened, after five years the bugger was on top of the pops, she now had to share her fiancée with millions of other girls. She married him, it was a public event; she bore his child, another public event. By the mid seventies she was living in a huge home away from all she had known in her youth. A mother of two daughters she saw little of Brian as he toured the world and of course there was the drinking, he always had liked a drop too much but now there was no stopping him. He was unfaithful and she knew it but hers was not the position of power in the relationship, though at times she was more like a mother to him. Then came the moods, terrible dark moods, as his career began to stall he became ever more bitter. He was always like that, either the biggest star in the world or a worthless no one; there was no middle ground with

Brian in those days. The whole Andy thing was a nightmare, an issue that she could at least see both sides of. Then it all went wrong and he was out, nothing to do all day but drink. She hid the kids away from him when he was at his worst and he had never taken out his problems on them. It was all over between them by the time he had his heart attacks but she had to see all that through, it wasn't that she didn't care, didn't love him, it had just become impossible. Now they had started coming to take things away from the house, things not paid for and the taxman, well that was another matter entirely.

By the end of 1983 Brian and Marilyn had split, the house was gone as were the horses and the boat; they were replaced by 33 Buttlehide, Mapel Cross, Herts.

Buttlehide is an arrangement of three council blocks, part concrete part brick designed in the late fifties. One of the blocks is beautifully situated facing a large open field, the residents grow window boxes; it's a very pleasant spot indeed, opposed to this block is a sister building which is no where near as nicely done but it's a passable residence for the inhabitants to live in. Brian was eventually moved into a ground floor flat in the third block. This block was thrown up next to a row of trees and bushes. It feels oppressive and isolated from the world. The view from Brian's tiny flat was of a bit of scrub-land partitioned off by a criss-cross wire fence.

Initially he was given a flat on the first floor but his knee problems were getting worse and worse so he asked the council on several occasions to move him to the ground floor. Eventually after his Dr confirmed his condition in writing and a ground floor flat became available Brian was moved. In early 1984 Frank Torpey left his large semi detached home in Harrow to meet his old band mate. "It was early in the year, like March, that didn't help but it was the place that did it, like Moscow it was, these terrible blocks at the top of a hill. He showed me in and gave me a cuppa tea he'd stopped drinking by then, even so his hands still shook. We chatted for ages about the old times and he said he was going to make it back somehow, you couldn't keep him down for long, not Brian; of course the funny thing was that half of his downfall was his own doing."

# It's all in the name

**Brian Connolly** "solo star" did not exist, his income as Brian Connolly would be tiny compared to what he could earn if he could use the word Sweet on advertisements for his act. One would think that it was a clear cut thing, he had formed the band, had sung on all its hits, he was without doubt the star of the Sweet. While this was the case, Andy Scott had other ideas.

Brian was by now on state benefits, living just above the poverty line, Andy had done much better but neither had hung on to the trappings of rock stardom. As the mists cleared and the dust settled it was obvious that only one thing could ensure they had any kind of future, work. Andy would argue in court that he had written most of the bands songs and produced many of them too. Following Brian's departure he had collaborated on a further four singles and three albums. Though they had all bombed commercially they counted as part of the Sweet's output. Some songs were credited to Scott alone; no material by Sweet was ever credited simply to Brian. The case dragged on for days and made the newspapers. Eventually the judge decreed that Brian could use the Title's The New Sweet or Brian Connolly's Sweet. Within a few years the case's precedent was adopted by Les Grey's MUD, Les Mcewans Bay City Rollers and by many other lead singers who had found solo success hard to come by.

Now that he could take advantage of the nostalgia market Brian began picking up the pieces of his career. From his little council flat he hatched a plan to claw his way back to fame and fortune.

He still believed in the dream of stardom, chart success and even the possibility of an acting career. The latter was never really on the cards, he seemed to possess no talent in this area. His adopted cousin had become a house hold name by the mid 80s in the TV detective drama Taggart. As Brian set out on the road for the first time in years with his New Sweet he needed publicity, he was long past the relevant stage with the music press who now saw him as a 'has been' who had once been in a novelty act. The regular press were sniffing around for scandal but other wise had nothing to report, it was six years since he was a famous star in the proper sense.

Brian needed an angle to sell to the press and so he found one via adoption and Taggart. The first few shows on his first tour sold out in hours, tickets were eagerly consumed by faithful fans starved of contact with their idol. From then on it was a hard slog to sell them and something had to be done. Brian was literally banking on this tour to pay the rent so he telephoned the tabloids and arranged some interviews he had a story to tell.

Mark McManus was an actor, he had grown up in Scotland he was a cousin by adoption of Brian Connolly. There was also another Mark McManus in the family who was an adopted brother of Brian Connolly. Neither was a blood relative of Brian.

By 1984 Brian's adoptive cousin was a house hold name, perhaps even more so than Brian had ever been. He had left Scotland in the mid 60s to live in Australia where he perfected his craft on TV shows such as The Ranger and Skippy the bush Kangaroo. In 1969 he returned to the UK to take a part in the movie Ned Kelly along side Mick Jagger. During Brian's heyday Mark was a jobbing actor appearing in episodes of police drama's and soaps until his big break came at the end of the decade with Taggart. Brian wasted no time in getting the "story" out there "Taggart is my Brother" screamed the headlines. "Taggart" was not pleased at having his fame annexed in this way, Brian's first New Sweet tour sold out.

With interest renewed a deal was struck with Anagram Records to release a compilation of Sweet's now quite ancient hits. It had been seven years since the failure of RCA's Golden Greats album and at last a package arrived with good cover art and most of the hits on board. With Brian touring the album made the charts and a public appearance was scheduled at a record store in London's Oxford Street. Steve flew in from New York, Mick attended looking ever youthful and Brian was pleased as punch, even demanding a wage from the record company at one point for his services in promoting the release. Andy could not be persuaded to attend any of the events surrounding the surprise hit. He had a new single out called 'Let Her Dance' and was banking on solo success after signing to the independent Static label. On the day of the signing hundreds of fans were present, lining the walls of the store and out into the busy street, to all it seemed like old times.

The dark days of heavy drinking and Baileys nightclub were long over and Brian was back in the spotlight.

# It's it's Sweet's hits ....
# another personal memory

**We** queued up to see them, as if we were kids once again, I was lucky to have found out in time, there was no internet then, a pal had seen an advert in the evening Standard and told me about the signing. The Sweet were at Tower records signing copies of their greatest hits LP, inside Sweet songs were playing over the Tannoy as I neared the counter. There they were, Brian, Mick and Steve. Brian looked old, Steve had put on weight and Mick, god he looked amazing, he had the looks, like a real rock star. I got to the desk and handed my LP to Steve, I've no idea what we said to each other. Then there he was Brian, the previous year he had shattered any illusions I may have had about him. He signed the thing and looked up at me, instantly there was recognition, "do I know you from somewhere?" he asked. I told him where we had met and to my amazement he remembered, he took hold of my hands and apologised profusely "I'm really sorry about that, I don't do that stuff anymore, ok" I was so happy, I no longer regarded them as the idols they once were, they were "past it" and I was growing up. He was just a man saying sorry to me, a very special man but a human being all the same. I asked if Andy would join them and he pulled an "I don't know" kind of face. He had lots more fans to see so I moved on but not before he once more gave me a nod that reiterated his regret at disgracing himself, he clearly was in recovery from alcoholism and working a program, I know that because within five or six years it would be my turn. I handed my LP to Mick who looked remarkable I knew he had lost his wife recently so I simply said that what ever happened I wished him health and happiness. I don't know how much of that crazy night Brian actually remembered, did he recall his "I can give you one" remark? I'll never know. To me as a gay man that's not really much of an issue is it ! I don't think it even says much about Brian's sexual orientation, he had played it camp for years' that's why as a little gay boy I adored him. I think he must have had so many passes made by gay fans and people who assumed he was gay that, well lets just say in that terribly drunken state his boundaries were all over the place. I don't really think he even knew what he was doing or saying, there was nothing remotely sexual in our meeting or our embrace that night; it was a fan and an idol that embraced. He also needed that special adoration badly, I adored him until that night and when I met him I fulfilled my absolute childhood dream. They were wrapped up and sold to us; Slade, MUD, Gary Glitter, even Marc Bolan. They were the very last of the glamorous rock stars and they were supposed to be adored by us and they were. At the end of the signing the press wanted pictures and Brian Connolly selected me, out of all those hundreds of fans he suggested I stand beside him. I was wearing a T-shirt I'd had made that said "Fuck Frankie I'm still into Sweet", at that time every body was wearing Frankie goes to Hollywood T shirts. A week after the event I was on the back page of NME with Brian Connolly and Steve Priest. So I met the two Brian's, the crazy one hell bent on destruction and the humble one trying desperately not to drink and to resurrect his career. The one thing that shone through both of them was vulnerability. A little while after the event I met Brian once more at Baileys in Watford, this time he was performing at the cabaret venue, he was sober, looked well and invited me to join him and his band for chicken and chips. As we chatted I became aware of a slight tremor in his hands and also in his voice. Otherwise he was warm, friendly and a little nervy about the approaching performance. He didn't really trust his voice and when I praised his singing he declared that anyone could sing better than him. To this day I wonder exactly how, as a fellow performer he could take to the stage possessing such a belief. During the performance later that night I got a little too close to the stage which was a rather low one that used to rise from the dance floor. A bouncer headed toward me and Brian signalled that the 'bruiser' should leave me be. I spent the final minutes of the gig perched beside Brian's monitor with my Sweet scarf held proudly aloft for the world to see. I was allowed to adopt this privileged position several more times over the next two or three years years.

153

**Abov**e. Brian Connolly, Brian Manly & Steve Priest, 1984, HMV Record signing (Photo Dick Barnatt)
**Below**, The Sweet mix makes the British top fifty in 1985

# The Ballroom Mix

**Within** weeks of the Sweet 16 hits album entering the charts plans were afoot to make a special single, a disco medley of Sweet's old hits. This was done using the new digital technology that made possible all manner of new edits and effects on the record. Titled Its It's the Sweet Mix the product was available in both seven and twelve inch formats. It entered the charts at a healthy number sixty five; Andy's 'Let Her Dance' had failed as had the follow up 'Krugerands', though unsurprisingly this title had been a hit in South Africa. Andy cuts a dashing figure in the pop video that promoted the song. A week later the Sweet single leaped twenty places up the chart to number forty five. It was agony for Brian, indeed for them all. Starved of fame and fortune for over half a decade it now looked very likely that they could be in the top forty within days and that could bring a call from Top of the pops. Brian's management immediately booked him on another nationwide tour, The Megga Tour. Since the success of the album Brian had been working in the studio on several songs, if he pulled it off and actually produced an album it would have taken him seven years! The premier track was called 'The Magic Circle'. After three weeks the Sweet Mix stalled at number forty five, had it shot into the top twenty it is likely that Scott and Connolly would have buried the hatchet and a Sweet reunion would have taken place, they each needed it badly but only if the price was right. It had been truly remarkable that Sweet had charted and album and a single after more than six fallow years but on week four the mix began to slide away to the bottom of the chart. The pressure on Brian was huge, if he did not secure a record deal now he never would again. Sadly Brian buckled under pressure and began to drink sporadically. This did not help progress with the album. In truth he stood very little chance of getting an album deal with any record company. He had no track record what so ever with regard albums, he had never had a solo hit single and his reputation as a drunk went before him. He was also forty years old and in "pop star" years this was more like ninety. It is a great shame that 'The Magic Circle' never found a taker, as it was the one song that could have provided Brian or Sweet with a hit by this time. It was hyper nostalgic, very 'Fox On The Run' in nature. Had the Sweet still been together the band would have been seventeen years old, most singles buyers of 1985 were not born during Brian's '70s heyday. The only way back would have been via the original audience who were now in their twenties.

Brian performed 'The Magic Circle' on The Mega Tour, always to great reactions from the crowd but as the months wore on it became clear that he had not been able to find a record deal. The song was shelved by the end of the year and did not re surface for a decade. Brian rightly believed that the number held the key to his chart fortunes. It is possible that the circle in the song was the joining of hands that occurs at the close of an AA meeting. Brian was attending meetings at this time and also appeared on one or two Sunday afternoon religious programs discussing his renewed faith in God. While he certainly had been developing a spiritual side to his nature it must be remembered that he would most likely have appeared on the Antiques Road Show or Police Five if they had booked him! Big Brother and reality TV was still a decade a way. Anagram had enough faith in the back catalogue to release a second Sweet Mix. Titled The Wig Wam Willy Mix it hovered just outside the charts for several weeks. At the close of the year it became obvious that despite using the last of his creative energy and physical stamina Brian's recording career was well and truly over. The only money to be made from recordings would be made from the old songs, with this in mind Brian went into the studio in mid 1986 to commit a crime that many a faded star has committed. Apart from the fact that his re recordings of the old sweet material were done very cheaply for budget release CDs, they suffered also because Chinn and Chapman had written the songs for a specific audience at a specific moment in a career. Brian was forty one years of age and his voice no longer suited numbers like 'Little Willy' and 'Poppa Joe'. He re recorded the entire Sweet singles catalogue for a company called Tring Music. These efforts hit the shops as a greatest hits of the 70s compilation in July 1987. Brian owned the rights to these re recordings and he hoped to earn a considerable amount from them but despite selling well in petrol stations and selected record stores they were soon forgotten. The rest of 1987 was a slog for Brian, he took his New Sweet to Germany and continued to work in the UK. Throughout 1985-6 and 7 the story about Taggart being a long lost brother would surface if the Connolly profile needed a boost, if not 'that' story then another angle was readily employed

"Sweet star broke in council flat" While these skirmishes with the tabloids may have provided him with large amounts of column inches in the national press they also degraded his image rather badly. By 1988 he was no longer flat broke but no longer looked upon as a glamorous star. His health was declining despite more than two years on the wagon. His hands now trembled virtually all the time, his head too. This also had an effect on his singing and spoken voice. The doctors seemed unable to diagnose any specific cause for his problems. Usually the body can repair itself from alcohol abuse given time, even at his age the process of decline should have at least been halted. It doesn't seem that his bout of infantile Meningitis was ever considered as a factor; having survived that in 1947 it is possible that the damage that occurred then had begun to manifest itself too. It may be that even without Sweet, stardom and alcoholism Brian would have experienced problems in later life. What is clear is that loading years of abuse on top of his childhood condition had certainly tipped his nervous system over the edge.

There would be one more attempt to reform the Sweet and it would be in America on the tenth anniversary of the bands break up. The break up occurred just as the bands members turned thirty years of age, so what did life hold for Sweets musicians? As the story itself lasts almost half a century, and the band was together for only a decade, the final years are split into four separate biographies so that each can take a final bow.

**Above**: Stewart Roney and Steve Priest celebrate the first tour of Steve's US Sweet in 2008. Stewart loyally runs the huge UK Sweet website

**www.sweet.com /HSH/**

# Stevie take a bow

**During** a decade in the public eye Steve Priest was unashamedly flamboyant, camp and out going. His contribution to the Sweet went far beyond playing Bass or providing excellent lead and backing vocals. He had a key role in the bands image from 1972 to 1977, singing his "special" interjections on all of the biggest hits. Never camera shy, Priest seems to have been born to play his role as Sweet's jester. If they no longer remember his name, the former 70s teenagers now approaching their fifties all remember, "the one who wore the make up" in the Sweet. Steve occupied his own special space in the pop universe for a while. His talent didn't stop at tomfoolery; he provided some epic vocal performances on the album Sweet Fanny Adams. "Restless" for example contains a vocal performance of the highest calibre. His Bass playing tended to be imaginative and faultless. Good as his voice undoubtedly was, it lacked that distinctive star quality that Connolly had in spades. By the time Connolly had been fired from Sweet Priest had all but assumed the role of lead singer. Thus as the band keeled over in a death throw, his personal fame was elevated in Germany where he sang the lead vocals on two minor hit singles.

He also sang most of the leads on the album Cut Above The Rest (April '79). This album was the long playing confirmation that a "Connolly- less"

Sweet would not be acceptable to the public. Its failure in even Germany marked the end of the road.

Despite the fact that Steve, Mick and Andy had contributed far more musically than Brian Connolly, they did not hold the key to the identity of the Sweet, ironically, 'Identity Crisis' was the final song Steve would work on while involved with a project still called Sweet.

Released posthumously in Germany the album Identity Crisis slipped quietly into oblivion, no singles were ever issued. There is a great performance by Steve on this little known LP, a cover of a song by Billy Boy Arnold call 'I Wish You Would'. By now Steve was living in New York and had started a band called The Allies. After more than a quarter of a century little is known of his project today. Later in the decade his song "Talk To Me' was featured in the movie Fast Food staring Traci Lords. 'Talk To Me' is quintessentially '80s and stands entirely on its own merit as a piece of work. It is his one famous song though it made little impact in the UK. In recent years he offered a CD compilation of his unfinished demos and recordings called Priest's Precious Poems.

Living an increasingly quiet life Steve's last work of note was the song 'Little Angel' that he co wrote and which featured on an album by the group Quiet Riot. Since leaving the band in 1981 he has had the least to do with all things Sweet. In 1984 he was tempted back to the UK to promote the chart hit album Its Its Sweet's Hits but when asked to accompany Mick Tucker and Andy Scott on a tour of Australia in mid 85 he declined with the comment "it sounds like slave labour". In 1988 he re-appeared with the band for some interviews and re recorded some of Sweet's early hits with Mike Chapman as producer. However when it became clear that the reformation was not going to materialise he shifted gear and delivered the song for the movie Fast Food. Since then there has been virtually no musical output from Steve. He self published an autobiography called Ready Steve some years ago in which he demonstrates his dry humour recounting his amorous adventures as a young rock star. Perhaps his own camp nature and his years as Sweet's "hotpant wearing tranny" are to blame for his tendency to recount his love of all things female and busty when ever the opportunity arises. From the middle of 1978 he seems to have had a battle with an ever expanding waistline, by the time the Sweet were promoting their final hit 'Call Me' he had pilled on the pounds and was sporting a thick moustache. The moustache didn't last long but the days of his svelte figure were long over by the 1980s. The last time Steve and Brian were on stage together was at Steve's eldest daughters wedding a year before Brian died. The number they performed was 'Uptight, everything is alright' by Stevie Wonder, just as they had done thirty years earlier in the Sweet Shop.

Known as the most laid back member of the Sweet, he settled in New York until the end of the 80s from where he re located to Los Angeles till the present day. During the 1990s he had business interests in real-estate amongst other pursuits. One of only two surviving members of the Sweet he is entering his 60s as a larger than life figure who until recently seemed contented with a quiet existence. In mid 2008 he surprised everyone concerned by forming an American Sweet. He has a web site and tours regularly in the US and Canada. It is not known if this is a response to the American property crash or a deep longing to play Chinnichap once more but by all accounts things are going well stateside for ole Steve and his version of Sweet. When contacted for his assistance in the production of this book he said "I wish you all the luck, it s about time someone told Brian's story" though he is a man of few words his replies were always swift and positive, so from me and the readers of this book I'd like to thank you and wish <u>you</u> all the luck in the world.

# Mick Tucker...A Very Nice Man

It is the norm in the music business that the lead singer is the spokesperson for a band, often followed hot on the heels by the lead guitarist. If one wanted a really good quote or turn of phrase where Sweet was concerned Mick Tucker could be most relied upon.

Mick hailed from North London, he was born Michael Thomas Tucker on July 17th 1947.

As a boy he had the normal childhood aspiration to become a professional footballer, instead he became one of the most famous rock drummers of the 1970s, it seems he was destined to "be something". Without him there would be no Sweet, he was a pillar of common sense and good will during the formative period with Brian Connolly. Largely self taught, his drumming technique and musical output have become well regarded amongst fellow percussionists the world over. Musicians, especially Rock musicians can be easily divided into personality types according to what instruments they play. Base Guitarists are usually laid back and steady, matching the sound of the instrument they play. Lead guitarists are egotistical, bright and have a sense of persecution. "Look at that bloody talent less lead singer getting all the attention when I am the one with all the talent" is a thread running through many a Rock magazine interview. In Andy Scott's case he also wrote and sang too.

Lead singers are paradoxically insecure and ultra egotistical, they inhabit the narcissistic domain of stardom; a world where gold can turn to a far more odorous substance over night. They exist not just to sing but to shine and to be adored. A stick is just a stick until the candy floss is added.

Drummers are often plain crazy. They do, after all, bash skins for a living. Percussionists like to make sudden loud noises while hidden behind a drum kit, placed well behind the action. Drummers are known for rash decision making and impulsive behaviour. Not like the lead guitar and vocalist peacocks, drummers are usually a macho breed, Rock music's equivalent to bodybuilders.

Mick Tucker was a gentleman, a softly spoken soul who could sing well and play some guitar. He was genuinely musical and effortlessly likeable. He loved being in Sweet, it has been described by him and others talking about him as "his life". Along with Brian and then Steve he began the journey from working class lad from north London to international rock star and thus turned what would have been a very ordinary life into a "dream come true".

During the five year period when he was seen almost weekly on British TV his charisma and boyish charm shone far beyond the confines of his drum kit. There was the customary twirl of drum stick when doing Top Of The Pops and of course in later years he contributed much to Sweets vocal sound. He endured much tragedy during his relatively short life, highs and lows that seem befitting to the personal CV of a "Star".

As his and Sweet's popularity began to falter in the late 70s his first wife Pauline died while taking a bath at the couples mansion home in Rickmansworth, just north of London. Press reports of the time suggest she had been suffering from depression and had fallen asleep while under the effects of medication. Today the press seems infatuated and obsessed with the wives of footballers, spouses who's own profiles outshine those of their famous partners.

In the 70s while there were celebrated rock chicks such as Brit Eckland and Marianne Faithful, the celebrity cult did not exist as it does today. Many quite ordinary girls were catapulted into another world after they married hard working Rock stars whose recording schedules and tour dates would keep them away for months on end. A five bedroom Victorian pile at the end of a long drive can seem like a dream home but to a young woman during long winter months it could also seem like an isolated nightmare. It is not believed that her death was suicide, simply a tragic accident. For Mick the hardest thing to live with was the fact that the tragedy occurred on New Years Eve while he visited a local pub to celebrate.

Mick continued to play in Sweet after Brian had departed. He had personally intervened on Brian's behalf when his colleagues decided that the singer had to go. Perhaps he had the insight, as a founder member of the band to see that it would ultimately not work without Brian.

Mick played on only one hit record that did not have Brian Connolly singing on it. 'Call Me' brought the spotlight just a little further his way in 1979. Sweet struggled on until a large tax bill, continuously falling sales and a general lack of enthusiasm brought them to an official ending in 1981. Mick married a lady called Jan in the 1980s and together they raised his daughter Ayston, the child of his deceased first spouse Pauline. Following his death Jan moved to Spain where she is by all accounts living in happy retirement.

In 1984 Mick enjoyed a Sweet renaissance with Steve and Brian. There was the top fifty album Its Its Sweet's Hits and also the hit single It's It's The Sweet mix. After six years out of the lime light in the UK it seemed the time was right for a reformation, if for no other purpose than to capitalize on the 17 year old group's nostalgia value.

Mick gave good, charming and intelligent interviews during this time and his smile showed that he relished another moment of pop stardom. the schism between Scott and Connolly at its all time low and with Scott poised to release some good new solo material, the moment passed without the four members of Sweet even being in the same room together.

In May 1985 Mick joined Andy Scott for a tour of Australia. With Steve Priest declining the invitation to join and Brian Connolly not welcome the tour was a success to some degree but a huge disappointment to the fans that, by and large, had allegiance with the original line up and in particular the star, Brian Connolly.

Mick continued to work alongside Scott for several years but the only real haven for the fractured Sweet was Germany, in Germany Sweet had outrun even Queen in their time. In the UK times were hard and the clubs small by comparison. There was work to be had, especially cabaret type shows and nostalgia shows but both audience and venue demanded Connolly, glitter and the early hits.

Mick last played drums with Scott in 1991. Ill health and a difference of opinion with the guitarist put an end to his musical career. His body of work is expansive, beginning with Slow motion in 1968 and not ending till "Its It's the Sweet mix" in 1985. Seventeen years of hits and significant record releases is an impressive legacy for a boy from Harlesden North London. The Sweet's lead singer wasn't the only member of the band to have a run in with the demon drink, Mick became a keen consumer himself but though at times he clearly had issues around his drinking and could go on wild booze binges he simply was not the same personality type as Brian.

During the early 90s Mick could be spotted walking the high street in Chorleywood looking every inch a rock star with his distinctive raven black hair permed teased and cascading over shoulders often clad in a black suit that could have been from a stage wardrobe. Presidents of the USA retain the title Mr President for life because of their outstanding contribution to the countries history. Mick Tucker remained in his mind and to his fans, a 'star' and he always turned out like one. Viewed through the eyes of a tabloid hack, Tuckers existence during the mid 90s could be reported as sad or deluded, singing in local pubs as he did occasionally and over dressing for a walk in a suburban town. It is easy to "knock" those who were once stars but is it reasonable or compassionate to do so without understanding. Mick Tucker loved being a star and as the decades went by he became ever ready for the pilgrims who trekked to Chorleywood armed with information on where he could be found.

Diagnosed with an aggressive form of Leukaemia in 1997 he fought a brave battle to survive and was indeed in a five year remission when literally overnight an opportunistic infection took his life at the age of 54. Above all other considerations in an amazing life, Mick was a thoroughly decent, kind and charming man who is greatly missed by all who knew him.

**Below**: Mick and Swiss fan Bruno in Chorleywood in 1987. Bruno recalls a lovely day after a chance meeting lead to drinks at the stars home and a warm welcome for him and his wife.

# Andy Scott...The Body of Work

**Bearing** in mind that he was the very last to join Sweet it is still no surprise that he is the last man standing at the helm almost forty years later. While Brian Connolly breathed Andy Scott could not become the icing on the Sweet's cake. The rift between the two had been deep and hate filled and had lasted for almost twenty years by the time Connolly's destroyed body finally quit living. Publicly Scott and several other sources claim that the two had made a peace in the weeks before Brian passed away, if this was so it would have been down purely to the obvious finale about to be played. No matter what he has said through the years since his wayward colleague died, messes Scott and Connolly were not ever going to perform on a stage again. The will was not there from Scott and the ability had long gone from Connolly.

If Brian's vocals had not been up to the job in either 1979 or much later in 1988, how could it possibly have been on the cards (as Scott maintains) that a Sweet reunion was just about to occur? By 1996 Brian's physical state was at the end of a decade of steady decline and his fate seemed inevitable.

Andy Scott's personal body of work is impressive in its sheer size and longevity. He had jumped on board The Sweet's coat tails little more than weeks before the release of 'Funny Funny'. Previously he had made much less commercial music, primarily with The Elastic Band and Mayfileds Mule at the end of the 60s. The outfit enjoyed little success but had been good enough to open for Jim Hendrix on not one but three occasions.

After joining Sweet and enjoying four years of stardom he began to widen his horizon, most of Sweet's material had not been to his taste and, like the others in the band he felt no special affection for Chinn and Chapman, despite the dozen hits they had provided.

His first project away from Sweet was a band he formed to produce and manage called Angel. Their first single appeared in early 1974 on Cube Records. 'Good Time Fanny' is a masterpiece of British Glam Rock/ Trash pop. Utterly brilliant from start to finish "Fanny" should have set the charts alight but was not sung by the right artists. Angel, a copy of Sweet had arrived two years too late if they wanted to ride the crest of the glam rock wave.

If 'Good Time Fanny' had been released by Sweet at any time in 1974 it would have been a big hit. Better than 'Teenage Rampage' musically, the guitar sound is as infectious as laughter. The heavily compressed sound is powerful, poppy and melodic; this was the moment of orgasm for glam rock after three years of teasing and heavy petting. A year later when 'Action' failed to maintain the momentum of 'Fox On The Run' Sweet would still have been wise to have re mixed 'Good Time Fanny' and put it out during Christmas 1975. The task would have been simple, remove the lead vocal, replace it with Connolly, re dub the guitar in one or two places where it sounds exactly like 'Teenage Rampage'.

Obviously the critics would have had a field day, Sweet cannibalizing the remains of a recent flop but this was the big difference between Chinn and Chapman and Scott's philosophy.

One doubts that Scott ever considered Using "Fanny" for Sweet, especially after the "serious" 'Action' was released. Yet the follow up to 'Action', 'Lies In Your Eyes' is a subtle steel of 'Fox On The Run' and the Rolling Stones number 'Satisfaction'. As with 'Fox On The Run', 'Good Time Fanny' sends sparks into the air. Slightly corny as happy songs always seem to be, Fox and Fanny put a smile on your face for three glorious minutes. The follow up by Andy's Angels was called 'Little Boy Blue'. Entirely different to its predecessor it is far noisier, less powerful and is only note worthy because elements of 'Fox On The Run' can be heard at the end of the song. Neither record was a hit for Angel in the UK, and they were heard of no more. There is a web site dedicated to them but this is purely because of their association with Sweet. The drummer on both singles was none other than Mick Tucker. One wonders if Angel were unhappy about not playing the instruments on their first two records, just as Sweet had been three years before.

Andy wrote a very nice song called 'Lady Starlight' which featured on the Desolation Boulevard album in August 1974. After the failure of 'Turn It Down' there was certainly a space in the chart for another Sweet related disc to be released and so following some re mixing and re recording 'Lady Starlight' became his first solo single. He performed it on several British TV shows including ITV's Supersonic but airplay was sparse and the disc failed to chart. It was a slow number and despite the falsetto vocals the arrangement was too masculine and plodded along slowly. Queen, for instance, would have added frills and occasional double beats to imply a quicker tempo. It was a good try but did not furnish Scott with any solo status. His outstanding contributions to Sweet's legacy are many though his indulgencies with regard solos and middle eight sections are littered across the bands musical landscape. One of the greatest examples of Andy "overplaying" is on the B side of his solo record 'Lady Starlight'. 'Where D'ya Go' is a pretty good melody for a B side, a simple song with a certain charm "lazing at home in my old rocking chair, listening to flip sides that got me know where", he sings happily in an early verse of the song. However the thing quickly turns into a prolonged guitar solo that destroys the integrity and structure of the song. At the very end of the track one can hear the voice of Mick Tucker scream "Bloody Shut up" from the control room. Obviously this was left in as a tongue in cheek gesture but guitarists are a breed best kept under control, less the issue of excess rears its noisy head. He is the only member of the band to get a credit for songs he had written entirely alone, 'Set Me Free' is widely considered a Rock classic today and its inclusion, along with 'Into The Night' on the album Sweet Fanny Adams gave the project both "Kick" and maturity.

Desolation Boulevard contains a real Scott treasure in the form of 'Medusa', the melody of which outshines all of the singles efforts post 'Fox On The Run'. Like 'Fox On The Run', 'Medusa' would have been a great single had it been produced in the same way, trimmed down, smoother and a fraction faster. As it is 'Medusa' is a fine song, the product of a man obviously at the top of his game.

No more solo numbers appeared until the LP Level headed in 1978, on this album he displays a rare glimpse of his softer side and it works beautifully. By becoming as heavy as they were in the late 70s Sweet had alienated many of their natural audience. For the first time in years Andy and Sweet were playing music that was essentially "pop".

'Dream On' and 'Fountain' in particular hit the mark for a mature but not necessarily rock enthusiastic audience. 'Love Is Like Oxygen' altered the course of the bands history and was a fitting if untimely finale to his and Sweet's mainstream career.

Like Mick and Steve, Andy struggled on with the Sweet as a three piece. It seems that it was he who really was not prepared to continue working with Brian Connolly.

There were three albums following Connolly's departure, each selling less than its predecessor. Undoubtedly the backbone of the Sweet's song writing structure, Scott demonstrated little skill as a "hit" merchant. Writing with the aplomb of Chinn and Chapman was beyond his capabilities within the single's market. However he had the talent in spades to provide first rate material for album releases.

Self production is very often a costly indulgence; very few ever reach their full potential in the arts while performing the task of both carrot and donkey. Many of Andy's songs had the potential to reach the wider public if they had they been produced by some one with a more commercial ear. Ultimately the best vehicle for his vehicles had been a ride on the "Chinnichap" express.

Just at the point of Sweet's demise in late 1980 Scott wrote a theme tune for a planned TV series, the resultant "Galaxy of Stars" was aired on two occasions but the show never took off and a single was never issued.

Around this time his marriage failed and he downsized considerably moving to a small flat in London's smart/trendy Maida vale.

In 1983 he signed a deal with Static Records and released several singles. 'Let Her Dance', 'Invisible' and 'Krugerands', the latter proved to be very popular in South Africa where it made the top ten.

Had a reformed Sweet done either of these numbers a ripple of chart activity would have been the likely outcome, purely because they were so different to Sweet's previous output. At the time, aged thirty-four one can fully appreciate Andy having one last try at establishing a name as a solo artist.

Having won the right to use the name Sweet in a court battle, Andy and Mick toured for some years using an ever growing roster of musicians to fill the ranks.

There have been sporadic albums using various vocalists the latest being an album called Sweetlife which was welcomed by the small but loyal community of his fans.

Recently Andy was reunited with his old school master, Mike Chapman while recording Suzi Quattro's first album in over a dozen years. Obviously not destined for the charts, the work was very well received and the title song 'Back To The Dive' received some selected radio attention.

Approaching his 60s the youngest member of the Sweet can look back at a long career that was triumphant yet flawed. The bulk of his reputation and success is built around some ten or twelve hit songs three of which were written by him.

In the US and UK the declaration that "we stand or fall under our own steam" was followed by a spectacular fall. In Germany things were very different and today he can fill medium size theatres and arenas performing with his current Sweet line up.

He has to live with failure each and every day of his life; it is the price to be paid for pop stardom, for pop stardom is not a job for life, being a musician is a job for life. He has publicly stated the mistakes made that de railed a career that would simply have run out of steam within a year or two, however two years could be six hit singles and a couple of gold albums in the record business.

Leaving Chinn and Chapman was a foolhardy move for they would have without doubt ensured that Sweet had more hit singles than any other band in the 70s, it was a simple mission. Sweet/ Smokie/ Sweet/ MUD/ Sweet/ Racey, the possibilities were endless, the pair made writing gold records look so effortless. It is easily possible to imagine Sweet performing Racey's 'Some Girls' in the same vein as they had 'Ballroom Blitz'.

At twenty-five Andy rightly believed he could conquer the world, he had almost done so with "Chinnichap" and now he wanted to demonstrate what really lay beneath his pop star image.

Both Sweet and Chinn and Chapman have endured derision and scorn from the ranks of Britain's musical establishment, insults and put downs thrown usually by critics who have not achieved even a fraction of the success enjoyed by Connolly, Chapman and Co.

Over the years since his commercial suicide Andy has shown time and time again that he was never a puppet or a product as such but at twenty-five and with the Chinnichap story only half way through in 1974 he can be forgiven for deserting one of the most successful song writing partnerships of the century.

Living luxuriously in a converted barn in Wiltshire, touring the nostalgia circuit and still producing occasional new works, Andy Scott is a proven survivor. Three decades on it is debatable how much difference five or six more hits would have made to him now. These days he is known to be a shade temperamental, (once called Her Majesty by Steve Priest) and not over keen on playing the older part of Sweets singles roster.

One of his more recent concerts in the UK was at Bilston in the North of England. The venue was very well attended on that night and the performance excellent. Both audience and players know who the Sweet were and indeed that this is not "it" but the musicians Scott picks to accompany him are a talented and savvy bunch, appreciating by and large that there are ghosts at every concert, both on and off stage. As a "brand" the Sweet turned forty in 2008 and it is almost certain that the last man standing will be Andy Scott.

Known as an uncompromising perfectionist, Scott all but fired Mick Tucker after the drummers drinking sprees began to affect his abilities behind the kit, a situation very reminiscent of the sacking of Connolly a decade earlier. Ousted from the very thing they had created neither of Sweet's former stars would live very long but both displayed great courage with their struggle to overcome ill health and feelings of devastation.

After a quarter of a century it is now very unlikely that the two surviving members of the Sweet will ever work together again. While retaining a dignified silence most of the time, Steve Priest has alluded that personal differences may be the cause.

# 2008 ~ A Personal Memory

**Quite** amazingly while walking in the street in 2008 I bumped into Andy Scott for the first time in my forty-year association with Sweet. I'd met Brian many times and Mick twice, I had met Steve at a record signing event but never had I met Scott.
I was bowled over for a moment and then introduced myself and told him of the up-coming book about Brian and Sweet. The conversation went like this:

"Wow, I was meant to meet you today, it s Andy isn't it "

"Yes, who are you?"

I told him about the project and that I'd sent a portion to him via his web site and had no reply. First he said he had not received it then he said he had but made no apology for totally ignoring me.

"Send it to me again and I'll look at it " he offered

"Ok, obviously a contribution would be great, oh and thanks for Good Time Fanny, I have loved it all these years, thanks for all the music, really"

"So what is this book then, some kind of scandal sheet or something?"

"Pardon?" I said taken totally aback

"You just dishing the dirt or something?" he said without a trace of emotion

"NO....no I'm not dishing the dirt, I just wanted to tell the story as no one else had and it's Brian and

Sweet's fortieth birthday soon, I wanted to put you in a context that was fair and pay my tribute"

"To Brian" he said

"Yes, to Brian, Mick, to you all"

"Send it to me and I'll let you know"

I shook Andy Scott's hand and left. I sent him the work once more and never heard a word. (Feb 09)

# Brian & Alcoholism
## (the final analysis)

By the mid 1980s Brian's fame in the tabloids was largely derived from his association with Taggart actor Mark Mc Manus. Both he and his "tabloid brother" were alcoholics, Brian desperately trying to remain in some kind of sober recovery, Mark seemingly hell bent on destruction via booze. A tragedy of such Greek proportions made such a good story that nothing was allowed to block its publication, not even the truth.

"Taggart star ashamed of pop brother antics" was a popular Sunday paper angle in the 1980s.

The waters are very muddied but according to Connolly's daughter Nicola in a late 90s interview, the two were not brothers or indeed relatives of any kind. They died within five years of each other though the detective's demise was through far more recent indulgences than the pop stars. Like all retractions Miss Connolly's corrective statement found far less column inches in the papers than the promotion of the myth had in the first place. With regard the assertion that the Taggart star was embarrassed by his fictitious brother's antics? He was probably annoyed at the total disregard that the "hacks" had displayed in telling the truth.

Alcoholism is a terrible but totally treatable disease, psychotherapy and recovery programs offer support and in some cases 'spiritual solutions' to the problem and can offer remedies almost resembling a cure. Brian Connolly had reasons a plenty to have become an alcoholic, his adoption issues, the pressures of fame, the pain of failure. One definite wrong turn in early life was his use of booze to steady him self just before he was to perform. Brian suffered from stage fright. To "cure" his trembling hands and terrible nerves he would have a few drinks before he went on stage. If there is one substance guaranteed not to cure nervous problems of any kind it is Alcohol.

The perception that alcoholism is purely a problem of over indulgence misses a crucial point with regard to the disease. It is not how much alcohol is consumed but much more importantly why and through what kind of need?

Alcoholism requires "dependency" from its subjects and Brian's using it as a form of tranquiliser set up a dependency right from the start. There are many who drink far too much, without becoming totally dependent on alcohol. There are also many who need far less alcohol to help them function but are unable to get by without it. The root cause is always some kind of dysfunction within the individual; unless the cause is treated properly the difficulties will only get worse.

Brian did not learn how to get over his nerves prior to his performance he washed away his feelings of fear with alcohol. Back in 1966 this would have been a common and frequently advised cure for stage fright Brian was doing nothing unusual. There is one crucial flaw in this approach to treating such a disorder; Brian did not learn how to cope using his own resources.

In March 1971 he achieved what he considered to be his destiny, all that knew him agree he clearly believed he would become a star.

Despite his issues with self-esteem Brian possessed that special belief that it would be him, against incalculable odds that would "make it"

It would seem implausible that a young man able to do this could also suffer from low self worth but there is an explanation for Connolly's escape from ordinary life into stardom. He believed in his dream rather than in himself or his capabilities as a singer.

In later years he confided that he thought almost anyone was a better singer than him. By this time his star had descended and his voice was long past its best but still, for a singer to have no belief in his own voice is an untenable situation.

From the start of his years as Sweet's lead guitarist it was clear that Andy Scott was a very talented man, not only talented but lucky too for he had joined a group who were about to have a hit regardless of whom the fourth member of the band was. 'Funny Funny' was in the bag no matter what, it was Brian's vehicle.

Pretty quickly it became clear that Scott could add a lot to the band, he was younger than Brian and had far more progressive ideas musically. Brian felt challenged and uncomfortable when Scott exerted his influence over Mick and Steve.

There were two tiers of discontent within the Sweet camp both running simultaneously. All four members resented the fact that they were entirely in the pockets of Chinn and Chapman, who made writing commercial hits look too easy to be believed. Brian and his band mates were all in their twenties and could not really grasp the impact their music was having on the lives of their young fans.

Chinn and Chapman were out to rule the decade; it was a publicly stated claim right from the start. While enjoying the fruits of Chinnichap Brian and his colleagues were not happy at all with the "pop act" aspect of their career. Yet they returned to the womb of Chinnichap on a dozen occasions to renew their tenancy on the UK and European charts.

Brian then resented the influence Scott had acquired in the band, more and more the songs wouldn't turn out the way he wanted them to.

Brian did not want his career hurling down the path of heavy rock and his insecurity simply fed from Scott's multitalented veins.

Conversely Andy had escaped the confines of ordinary life by joining a group he wouldn't have given the time of day to as a paying customer.

Brian was not particularly musical, he was a singer and as a singer he had been blessed with the ultimate gift a singer can have, a highly distinctive voice. The Sweet would never have gotten off the ground without Brian, he had the looks and the voice and they were what had sold The Sweet and 'Funny Funny'. However external success does not cure internal turmoil or insecurity.

As Brian soon found out fame is an elusive and high maintenance mistress to keep.

From the moment 'Alexander Graham Bell' stalled on the charts Brian's time as natural leader of The Sweet began to come to a close. He understood the kind of melody they had been dealing with so far, everything from Slow Motion to 'Poppa Joe', good commercial pop for the pin up singer to convey. One only has listen to the ease with which Brian sings the first thirty tracks he recorded to see that he is in his professional element. He has total command of his pitching, phrasing and delivery; his performances are extremely good Brian clearly knows what he is doing. It was both a blessing and a curse that within his vocal chords Brian had several different voices, his voice distorted beautifully into a gravel tinged brogue when under pressure in the higher range. As a smoker he also made the texture of his higher range more ragged and masculine, however like most "singing smokers" he was apt to sing flat in the lower register. These aspects of his voice combined with years of smoking would cause him many problems in later years but during the early part of his career his voice was superb.

Mike Chapman had a keen ear when it came to his artist's capabilities and the songs he would write around them, he set about inserting lines in verses or entire choruses that allowed Brian to belt at full throttle. 'Wig Wam Bam' is a perfect example of Connolly soft and Connolly hard all on one record. This trend continued culminating with 'Teenage Rampage', which was very problematic for Brian to sing, tears were shed in the studio as he became hoarse from what is little more than screaming in places. Solace was again found within the contents of a bottle of Whiskey and a packet of Cigarettes, undoubtedly the worse things that can be inflicted on a set of highly stressed vocal chords.

Other downsides for the singer to contend with were the pressures of simply becoming "that" famous. Imagine being a young Heterosexual man, twenty eight years of age and wearing more make up than your wife. Now add 'Blockbuster' to the equation and a situation occurs that is beyond most people's imagination. Most actors and singers portray some kind of "image" to the public.

Rock Hudson, Hollywood beef cake and romantic lead to Doris Day in several movies was in fact a man with a penchant for well endowed Muscle boys and sadly became a casualty of Aids during the mid 1980s. To his legions of female admires the truth would have been unthinkable in his closeted heyday.

Brian Connolly, formerly McManus, was a married man, heterosexual and not particularly effeminate in nature. In 1973 his performance and stage attire were outrageously effeminate, camp and to all intents and purposes hyper Gay. Yes Gary Glitter had jumped over the top too as did Marc Bolan, David Bowie and several other acts of the time but Sweet actually played at being outrageous queens. Gary Glitter had a massive following of working class boys, his music was "blokey" with its chants and invitations to punch the air and clap along in time. Like wise Slade had a huge following of working class boys who still considered the lads as "hard" despite Dave Hills excessive stage spangles and Cleopatra hairstyle. Marc Bolan and David Bowie were the 'real thing' in the androgyny stakes, they truly revelled in and understood the sexual waters they were so happy to muddy. One cannot imagine them caring a hoot what people thought about their sex lives, indeed both professed to be bi sexual, then heterosexual, then a sexual and possibly Pan sexual to boot!

Brian Connolly however was a far more normal kind of chap, underneath the mascara, foundation, glitter vests and a yard of yellow blow-dried hair stood a regular guy. The country and western singer to be, the wannabe movie actor was now totally incongruent with his public image and the reaction it produced almost twenty-four hours a day. Catcalls, wolf whistles and occasional insults were thrown at each member of the band but none was more famous than Connolly. Simultaneously he was stalked and adored by the readers of magazines such as Jackie. Girls adored his androgenic aura from the beginning just as they had Bolan and Bowie too.

Had Brian been gay it may have been easier not to mention more genuine, though flying this fast through the universe is usually unsustainable for all but the toughest of icons. So in a period of just under ten years Brian had discovered that his early life had been a sham and his identity shattered, then he had become a famous pop star and then for one year during 1973 he had become a glitter festooned celebration of all things queer. Only Steve out did him in this respect but none of Sweet was more famous than Brian, he bore the brunt of it all.

Brian experienced two huge dilemmas of incongruence, the Connolly McManus factor and the public portrayal of a personality nothing like his own. Stars often meet a public that has formed an opinion of them based on news paper articles and such like but players in The Sweet had hoodwinked most of the northern hemisphere into believing them to be far 'stranger' than they really were. As a band Sweet expressed the whole dilemma perfectly on the b side of The 'Ballroom Blitz' with the song Rock and Roll disgrace.

Brian had a long marriage to his first wife Marilyn, his daughters Nicola and Michelle were born in 1975 and 1977 just as his recording career began to fail. He and Marilyn had been together since his early twenties and it is she more than anyone who witnessed and experienced the effects of Brian's issues around his adoption and career. Today there is a wall of silence surrounding his family who are no longer willing to talk about him publicly.

All three of Brian's colleagues agree on one thing, he took little part or interest in the writing of Sweet's songs after 'Fox On The Run'. On a purely musical front there was a total disagreement on direction and style from that point on. In later years Brian confided that he particularly liked the ultra melodic nature of 'Fox On The Run' and felt that they (sweet) could have repeated that exact feel several times over on subsequent singles. They had discovered another "trade mark sound" he believed but then moved on to 'Action' rather too quickly abandoning the emotive singsong rock formula. By the time a U turn was taken with 'Lies In Your Eyes' the moment had passed and any way 'Lies In Your Eyes' lacked any sort of sing song chorus.

A further Incongruence almost unique to Brian and Sweet was the difference in their stature and popularity on mainland Europe compared to in the UK. Most artists have hot spots and dead spots during their careers. In Germany Brian and Sweet were a true Phenomenon. Brian would get on a plane in Hamburg, running a gauntlet of screaming fans and arrive in Luton or Gatwick with a bump, at the end of 1976 his face was conspicuously absent from the UK's TV screens and teen magazines, no one wanted to know. Obviously it was a tough call for Andy, Mick and Steve too, especially after the declaration that "we stand or fall on our own from now on", however they had not been half as famous as Brian with regard the pin up aspect of Sweet.

While the pressures of fame are many, the pressures of failure are greater still. In 1977 all of their peers were suffering a tremendous downturn too. Slade's biggest hit of 77 was a cover version of "My Baby Left Me" which got to number thirty-two. Marc Bolan had no hits but his TV career was blossoming and he had signed to do another series of Marc, his Thames TV show shortly before his tragic death in a car accident.

Sweet were in a self-inflicted exile, no tours, no concerts and no hits during 1977. As an alcoholic this would have affected Brian's ego badly indeed. Most people who exhibit the kind of problems he did, experience two opposing "ego states", Brian was all at once a big headed show off superstar and a wretched talent less fake.

To compound this by 1977 he was also a "has been", a thirty two year old pop pin up whose records no longer sold and whose picture was no longer in the papers. He had missed his prime moment to jump ship and begin a solo career, even a compromise had not been made by where he had released a solo single while remaining in the band.

Although Sweet had recently enjoyed great success in America it had been with the groups back catalogue. In the US the common belief is that Sweet split with Chinnichap at some point in 1976 not 1974. All Sweet's eight successes stateside had been released retrospectively to some degree. 'Little Willy' had been a hit of July 1973 and then The 'Ballroom Blitz' had restored the band in 1975. 'Fox On The Run' had followed at the end of the year while 'Action' had reached number fifteen in 1976.

American success aside, the game was up in 1977, three flop singles in their home land and a loss of acquaintance with the man on the street had left Brian Connolly and his Sweet hi and dry. This would be testing for the ego of any former star but for an alcoholic such as Brian this humiliation would have been intolerable.

If his condition is for one moment left to one side, Brian Connolly looks like a fool, an ungrateful, drunken, unfocused fool.

He and indeed the other members of the band at least owed the British fans a concert or two; these were fans who had stuck by the band all the way into oblivion, mounting campaigns for Airplay at radio stations, writing to TV producers demanding Sweet be given a chance to play.

Despite this out pouring of love and devotion from his remaining British fans, Brian loped around in Gerards Cross downing a bottle of scotch before lunch.

Of course there are always the moralisers who will have no truck with those who succumb to addiction and mental health problems.

However it is universally accepted that the person most damaged by the actions of an Alcoholic is the Alcoholic him self.

Fools do not damage and destroy themselves, sick people do, very often people who have seemingly to conquered the world. Perhaps they sought to make themselves feel secure by becoming so successful that "nothing could touch them". No such state exists and if there is one area of life that is furthest away from "security" it is show business. A gold disc is no substitute for psychotherapy and in 1977 RCA were about to let Sweet go.

Obviously exhausted, the writing team of Connolly, Scott, Tucker and Priest did not write the next Sweet single, instead the hit was written by the intruder, the Cuckoo in the nest, the thorn in Brian's side, Andy Scott. It was in truth just what the doctor ordered; they had previously been putting out records that were a variation on a rapidly diminishing theme.

It is clear from all commentators that by 1978 the atmosphere between Scott and Connolly was deadly. Neither fully appreciated that their career almost totally depended on the other.

Scott the perfectionist had total contempt for Connolly the drunken clown, this bad feeling, mutual on both sides would only have made Brian's behaviour worse, an Alcoholic and a resentment make lousy company.

At this point in the Sweet's story the end seemed inevitable. Brian's voice had suffered badly from years of abuse, cigarettes and whisky alone will do terrible damage but Brian had also been forced to sing at the edge of his range for several years. He had also been taken into musical territory that his instincts did not fully understand. Often a recording session for him was a process of learning not only the songs but also how to phrase and sing them. It is to his credit that some of his performances on the final Album with Sweet, Level Headed are powerful and heartfelt.

By the end of the year the band had split and Brian was teetering on the Abyss of living hell. In February 1979 Andy Mick and Steve announced that they were now a three piece and that Brian was going solo.

He was in fact going nowhere at all. Without the structure of work commitments Brian came apart at the seams. Every doubt and fear from his past would have plagued his sober moments; he had resolved nothing during his tumultuous years as a pop star.

As Andy, Steve and Mick went to Germany with 'Call Me' to take a final bow Brian consumed amounts of alcohol that would have killed a lesser mortal.

Financially he was in free fall, his income had dried up, his expenses were huge and the taxman had only just gotten around to calculating his liability for the big years of his career. In those days the highest rate of tax in the UK was a staggering 98%. His voice could still recover when rested and his efforts on 'Don't You Know A Lady' were heroic but he simply did not have the focus or the stamina to mount a come back proper. Musically at this point he was way off course but considering the direction of his life in general, it goes without saying that he would have been virtually impossible to advise or manage.

Denial is Alcoholism's greatest friend, without denial the disease cannot progress and inflict further damage. Brian was in total denial at this point, surfacing briefly, assessing the damage and then drowning it all out again. When he was dropped by Polydor records in late 1980 this would have been the final straw, a paltry two singles in eighteen solo months and now he was without a recording contract for the first time in twelve years.

After a year at the edge he slid into the Abyss of addiction sinking as low as it is possible to go. Alcoholism is a progressive disease the progression occurring exponentially, the worse "it" got the worse "he" got, he was literally sinking.

# Rock Bottom

**Rock** bottom in alcoholic terms is when a prospective "patient" reaches a point just before death but shortly after all other options have been exhausted. It seems that while there is still some room to manoeuvre the addict will continue using their substance of choice. Sadly this can go beyond the point of no return and as a result there are many thousands of deaths each year from alcoholism in the UK.

Brian's weight ballooned during 1980 and by early 81 he became unrecognisable as the slender star from the previous decade. Two years of virtual inactivity and days of consuming calorie laden alcoholic drink had resulted in his weight reaching almost fifteen stones. He simply loosened his belt, had his trousers taken out and carried on. His denial was so strong that all physical aspects of his illness were ignored. His hands would tremble in the morning and he has admitted that the amount of Whisky required to stop these tremors was incalculable in "pub measure" terms.

While his treatment at the hands of Andy Scott regarding Sweet may not have been particularly kind, Brian made no real effort to see the true reasons for his demise. Bitter and raging he lived in a twilight world of self-loathing and drunken rages. He could be obnoxious when drunk just like any other alcoholic but his humiliation was far more public than ordinary folk can imagine. Any fan approaching during this time, inquiring as to what he was doing now or what his plans were could receive a nasty shock from their former idol.

Self pity is not the sole preserve of the alcoholic; they simply do it better than almost anyone else. The first rule of therapy and counselling for addicts is to stop blaming others and look only at your part in your downfall, Brian was not yet at this point but he would be soon.

After a particularly heavy drinking spree in 1981 Brian became quite unwell, it was touch and go that night but the man who sang 'Blockbuster' survived. This was the beginning of two new phenomena regarding Brian Connolly; the relentless decline in his physical state and a stubbornness of character that demonstrated his iron will, a 'will' few could have imagined he was capable of.

It is possible for an addict to recover totally from addiction with one proviso; they must never use the substance they were addicted to again. The mind can be altered in many ways but once the body itself has developed a tolerance there is no turning back.

It is not clear how soon Brian really started to get to grips with his alcoholism after his brush with death. It is said that he attended AA and had some counselling. It is clear that his life slowly began to turn around after that night on the edge of death.

Brian had wanted to deliver singsong pop numbers with a country tinge but actually now released the heaviest single of his entire singing career. The recording of Hypnotised was very problematic, Brian was still on the mend, indeed it was his near fatal health crisis that had spawned the good will for the record to be made.

The following year was not a good one for Brian. It was now obvious and more acceptable to him that he was not a solo star and his name alone would not earn him a living. Far more than a "living" was required at this point if he were to avoid bankruptcy. In January 1983 he supported American Rock star Pat Benatar on her UK tour performing four gigs. The most prestigious of the dates was without doubt the Hammersmith Odeon show on January 22nd. Almost five years to the day since Sweet had triumphed at the venue while high in the charts with 'Love Is Like Oxygen'. Brian returned as the support act to Benetar who although very esteemed and critically acclaimed, had nothing like the fame Brian had enjoyed in the previous decade. At the point of their tour together Benatar had yet to make the UK charts and when she did her success was meagre indeed, the pinnacle of her singles output being Love Is A Battle Field written by none other than Mike Chapman, it reached no 17 in 1985. Brian's work with the Diva was not triumphant and only served to confirm that he needed to re structure his career and his aspirations if he were to survive. On the tour he had a good band known as either The Brian Connolly Band or Encore, the two main players were Terry Utley, (Smokie) and John Verity who had written and produced Hypnotised. Brian's dalliance with Miss Benatar saw then end of Brian Connolly the solo singer. Naturally there were plenty of Sweet fans in the audience to cheer him on but by March 1983 it was obvious that this was not going to be the way forward.

He and Marilyn were living all but separate lives, while most of the trappings of his former stardom had been re possessed or sold.

Without his former colleagues Brian's career as a serious pop artist had never materialised. He had released only six songs in five years and these were not a cohesive body, they were bits and pieces salvaged from his moments in the studio.

Brian busied himself writing new material while also promoting compilation albums. His voice was in bad shape but amazingly he turned in some good performances while trying to construct a solo album called Jailbait. The songs "Red Haired Rage" and "The Final Show" still exist in demo form and are very reminiscent of his days with Sweet.

At this point in time Brian had a fairly firm grasp on his recovery from alcohol. The wreckage of his life lay all around him but with amazing strength he began "sifting" with a new purpose and energy.

He went back on the road and it was there that the public began to notice that all was not well with Brian Connolly.

Barely detectable, as he signed albums and chatted to fans was a tremble in his hands, a prelude to terrible problems that lay just around the next corner, a vague tremor, almost imperceptible.

Brian had always been a nervous type, especially on TV or stage so few really appreciated the significance of this new nervous tick, he looked better than he had in years, he was off the booze and for a while the future looked bright for the man who sang 'Blockbuster'.

During the recording sessions for his final try at a pop comeback he was having new problems with regard the vibrato in his voice.

All singers who employ large amounts of vibrato in their vocals tend to suffer from an exaggeration of this "wobble" as they grow older. Singers who smoke are especially prone. They often employ vibrato as a method of pitch adjustment, a way of avoiding singing flat in the lower register or of resisting the highest notes during a particularly difficult part of a score. Vibrato tends to increase with age because the vocal chords have become less taught and it is harder for the singer to "steady" the pitch of their voice. If a singer has no natural tendency toward Vibrato their voice will often become "thinner" with age.

Having been back in the chart again with the greatest hits album must have been wonderful for Brian, Mick and Steve.

The sweet had charted an album in the United Kingdom for only the second time in thirteen years yet its four members could not be persuaded to pose for so much as a photograph. For some reason the heart had begun to beat again, the patient was alive! Sadly seizing the opportunity would require more tolerance and forgiveness than either Connollly or Scott could muster. After the Sweet mix left the singles chart in early 1985 there would never again be the interest or real opportunity to re launch the Sweet into the public domain.

It really had been a miracle that Sweet was back in the top fifty at all.

Brian's mega tour of spring 85 was a huge success but not enough to save him from financial ruin. Creditors including the Inland Revenue were held at bay by the promise that a recording comeback would provide the amount needed to clear his debts. There was one song from his recent clutch of recordings that had the potential to change everything. 'The Magic Circle' is Brian's greatest solo work; Brian had amazingly infused a Chinnichap like quality into this pastiche of one of Sweet's songs. Had Sweet re formed at this post Mega mix juncture and released a better version of 'The Magic Circle' they could have had a hit. As the Drummer and guitarist were on a tour of Australia and the Base player had taken up residence in New York, a reformation was out of the question. It is unlikely that the rest of Brian's former band mates would have wanted to have been associated with the "corny song" as they would almost certainly have lacked the overview at this point in their lives to appreciate that a nostalgic pastiche was all the wider public would tolerate from a band in its seventeenth year, a band whose last hit had occurred eight years before. How can a musician in there thirties accept that they will always be seen as a thing of the past?

In 1987 Brian's act changed its name to Brian Connolly's Sweet and a new dimension of touring came into play. Through the years Andy in particular has tried to distance himself from The Sweet's connection to Nicky Chinn and Mike Chapman. Time and time again he has made comments such as "in Britain we were lumped in with MUD and Suzi Quattro but in the rest of the world we were seen as something totally different"

Sweet were, without question a Chinnichap act, Sweet's total weeks in the UK chart add up to one hundred and fifty seven of which one hundred and twenty nine were with Chinn Chapman compositions.

In Germany Sweet did have a longer post Chinnichap decline, one that leaves a different statistical legacy for sure but seven of their eight number ones were written by Nicky Chinn and Mike Chapman.

By the end of 1987 Brian Connolly's Sweet were struggling to find well paid regular work. There was an audience out there, the average Sweet fan was by now pushing thirty but it was becoming harder and harder to reach them. Andy and Mick were suffering the same problem, especially in the UK where work was hard to find and in some very small venues indeed. Brian teamed up with Les Grey and MUD to tour the UK at selected venues, so successful were the two together that plans were made for a larger national tour.

At the start of 1988 Brian was moved to a ground floor flat in Maple Cross, his finances were off of the buffers, though he had little more than the average man in the street, a council flat, a nice car and a job in the evenings that brought in good money. The move was because he was having problems with the two flights of stairs at his other address. To add to his woes an old knee injury was once again giving him problems.

In April the telephone rang bringing an offer, an offer to re form The Sweet. At forty-three and in his circumstances he had little trouble accepting the deal and jumping onto a plane to California.

There assembled were all the old players, Andy, Mick, Steve, and Mike Chapman.

They were there to re record five of the bands previous hits, always a perilous undertaking after the passing of many years.

Announcements were made that "we" are back together and "Sweet were ready to take on the world again" but the moment had passed in 85. A compilation of the bands heavy rock cuts had been issued in August 1987 called Hard Centres and it has been favourably received despite having no impact on the charts. Brian was over forty, the others following not far behind, they had not been famous in the true sense of the word for a decade. These factors aside, Brian was not up to a comeback on the scale being planned, either vocally or in purely physical terms. Interviewed along with the rest of the band at Tower Records in 1988 his head trembles throughout the interview. The general atmosphere between the band members is more akin to a wake rather than a re birth. Andy, when asked what he has been doing for the last ten years omits to pat him self on the back by just saying "I had a big hit in south Africa with the song Krugarands".

Instead he simply states that he has had some success abroad.

Steve too was over "cagey" and went from sounding pretentiously enigmatic with his "this and that" description of his work during his decade in the wilderness to self- deprecation with his statement that "none of it got anywhere". The dynamic feels wrong when the interview is seen today. It is, like so many other clips, available on the Internet. Brian's limitations aside, the "band" does not appear to be a cohesive unit in the interview.

In the studio in LA with Chapman at the control panel Brian didn't stand a chance, a consummate professional, slave driver and perfectionist Chapman was dismayed at the decline of his one time prodigy's health and ability to sing.

Add to this a very sceptical Guitar player, who had not deemed Connolly's work up to scratch nine years previous and Brian's chances of passing "the audition" were slim to say the least.

'Action', 'Ballroom Blitz' and 'Fox On The Run' were all re created but the resultant tracks were deemed unusable due to Brian's performance.

Had there been love in the band instead of feelings bordering on hate a compromise could easily have been struck. Till the day he died Brian still had the ability to impersonate his catch phrase vocal characteristics. Material would have to have been written directly with his problems in mind. These accommodations occur on a daily basis in the music business especially with older singer's whose instrument is after all flesh and blood. At forty-three Brian had the voice of a sixty year old. Studio problems aside Brian would not be able to withstand the rigours of a full US tour.

To load the failures of this attempt to re float Sweet all on Brian's shoulders would be very unfair indeed. Sweet were now totally unknown to the younger generation who would have seen them as something purely from the past. While in the studio working on the songs Brian popped out for a packet of Benson and Hedges and managed to get him self lost for over an hour which apparently did not go down well with the band who wrongly assumed he had perhaps fallen off the wagon. More telling is the fact that he needed to nip out for Cigarettes, tobacco and nicotine are terribly damaging to the vocal chords and it will always be a great pity that Brian never managed to stop smoking. More then anything else, it was probably the cause of his voice deteriorating to the extent that it did.

Despite his mounting physical problems and his abilities as a singer in great decline Brian had hoped against hope that a reunion would be possible. Just one year together as Sweet would yield them all a great deal of money but more than that he wanted to feel the sensation of standing before a crowd of screaming fans again.

He frequently stood before six or eight hundred very enthusiastic people at his shows but as he put it "the buzz for the four of them would be amazing" The mist finally was really clearing from his mind but with the clarity came the realisation that it was probably over, he was forty three, a little old to be a pop star all over again.

# Sweet's 'Ballroom Blitz' Video

**The** teasing with regards a full reunion of Sweet continued for another six months and culminated with the release of the Castle Hendring Video, Sweet's 'Ballroom Blitz' in 1999. Once again the fans were treated to some appalling psychological "Jiggery pokery" during the interviews between the hits.

Here is a band purporting to be on the verge of a Million dollar comeback with 1990 to look forward to yet the guitarist declares that "You don't have to love the people you work with" worse still the Base guitarist does not deem the re launch video important enough to take part in. Perhaps he had already decided the previous year that the game was well and truly over.

Poor Brian on the other hand is almost moved to tears when describing how "amazing" it is going to be and how a lot of people are "not going to believe that it's actually happening". There were many reportedly sad moments in Brian's public life but his yearning for Sweet to re unite and his belief that it really would happen was truly sad and very hard to witness. During the video he finds it impossible to disguise how emotional he feels.

The video did very well, the comeback did not, in fact it never materialised at all. Still in his council flat but financially "out of jail" Brian made a wise decision to change the structure of the band he worked with and employ them as "waged" backing musicians.

The name underwent its final change and from1991 Brian's act was known as BCs Sweet. Through out the 80s Brian had used the Sunday tabloids as a way of keeping his name in the public eye. The old adage "all publicity is good publicity" is not strictly true. Each thought the other had the upper hand but tabloid fame is a ghastly aberration and ultimately cheapens all it touches.

"Sweet star in council house" Sweet Nothing's" "Sweet heartache" on and on went the pun laden headlines as Brian collected his fee for another public humiliation, each tabloid excursion de valuing his currency just a little more. Often the stories were of planned comebacks and million pound deals but nothing ever came of any of these offers.

In 1990, with the new Compact Disc format now becoming big business Brian seized a new opportunity and re recorded three hits from his back catalogue with Sweet. Hits of the 70s was a box set CD offering of new versions of songs by artists such as the New Seekers, the Rubettes and the Glitter band. Because of a disclaimer on the cover Brian recorded under the Sweet banner for the first time in twelve years. The disclaimer on the cover states that the re recordings were done to improve the quality as the original recordings were very old.

There certainly was no need to re record a single note of anything mastered after the mid 60s. The reason was purely financial, for although Brian, Andy, Mick and Steve would never earn a writer's royalty from the bulk of their hits they could earn performers royalties via mechanical copyright. Brian re recorded the songs with session musicians so that all performance royalties from these particular versions would be his. They are not good versions on any level; cheaply made and poorly produced they were in circulation for only one or two years. No effective techniques were employed to camouflage how old Brian sounded or how unsteady his voice was at times.

In 1990 Andy and Mick took off on a tour of the United States and Canada. Andy had gained some weight at this point while Mick still looked amazing for a man of forty-one. The age problem for Sweet in particular stems from the Chinnichap period of 1971-73. The material is totally bespoke for youthful players and a youthful audience. It would never be "credible" for Brian to re record his repertoire at the age of forty five, he had been a little long in the tooth for such teeny bop material aged thirty but he had pulled it off. There was virtually nothing in Sweet's roster of hits that had been built for older performers to deliver. Credibility was by 1990 a high-minded concept for the struggling members of the once mighty Sweet.

**Above:** Super fan Cos Cimmino and Brian Connolly in 1994 Brian aged 48. Cos runs the Sweet Fanzine Cut Above The Rest.

**Cutabovetherest.org.uk**

# Monsters of Glam

In 1990 and 91 there were two events held in Norfolk to celebrate all things 70s and Glam Rock. Brian had gone down well at each event held at Pontins holiday centre. The "Hemsby Glam Rock Weekend " re united Brian with his old pal Les Gray who, like Brian was touring with backing musicians under the name Les Grays MUD. Always friends as well as rivals the two were delighted when a promoter offered to finance a major tour of the UK with each of them sharing top billing and performing a ten number set. While neither "incomplete" band could fill enough theatres for a full tour by the 90s, together they certainly did have pulling power.

The first tour was called Monsters of Glam rock and it found Brian performing better then he had in years. Basically he had learned how to impersonate himself. Once the audience had had a moment to get over the shock of his haggard appearance, trembling hands and slow approach to the mike stand they were in for a treat because the moment the mike was in his hand Brian came alive.

At forty six he could still have looked youthful, he was in fact a semi invalid who found being Brian Connolly very exhausting, though that didn't stop him. Some nights he was last on stage, on others Les closed with 'Tiger Feet' allowing Brian an early get away to his hotel bed. Two aged stars were delivering Chinnichap heaven to an audience of "thirty something" fans. Nostalgia is a relative concept; Brian had been a contemporary star for little more than seven years, as a nostalgic icon he was now in his second decade!

By 1993 Brian would join forces with Suzi Quattro, MUD, The Glitter band and any number of lesser known 70s artists on tours in Europe and across the UK. He was not wealthy and still lived in his council flat but ran a nice car and could buy what he wanted within reason. He had re recorded most of the Sweet's back catalogue but the results were dreadful. He was a performer, a star, not a producer or songwriter. There had been no new material released for eleven years and he rarely strayed from his set of ten Sweet hits unless it was to add a favourite cover version. One such song was the Stevie Wonder classic Uptight (everything's alright). These additions occasionally had people in the audience perplexed as they would not have known that Brian had been a consummate Motown merchant during the late sixties.

Had he been in better health the future would have looked comfortable but he was aging at three times the speed of a normal man and he knew it. As the summer of 1993 came to a close he was begging to tire of his life screaming catch phrases such as "Look Out" and "Lets Go" but he had to go on. His children were not yet fully grown and although he had not been able to provide for them at times when he was younger he had done his best in the 90s with his new found solvent status.

In 1990 Brian married his partner Denise but the marriage ended in divorce after four years, by the time the divorce had actually come through Brian was living with the woman who would become his final partner and mother of his only son.

Brian and Jean were together for just over two years and it was during this period that Brian became the proud father of a son duly names Brian James Connolly. During an interview in 2007 Frank Torpey recalled a wonderful exchange between him and the late Mick Tucker: "I remember I said to Mick one day that Brian's new girl friend was a hairdresser and Mick shot back that ""they were all bloody hairdressers!"

Having a child may seem like a 'Crazy' thing for an ailing middle aged pop star to do but the timing couldn't have been better in terms of Brian's finances. Brian had now gained total control of all merchandise sold at BC Sweet gigs. He had seen how much could be made while on a short tour of Germany. Many products could be made and sold for a fraction' of the price of making an album and indeed the public saw such items as little more than additions to hot dogs or pop corn and were eager to buy them. T-shirts pens and badges were all printed and sold at his shows along with signed photos. Signed photos could be a bit of a problem for Brian; especially as his tremors grew worse so many such signed pics were actually signed by members of his band, simply with the message "With thanks B. Connolly." To this day there must be some members of the public who believe that they have the genuine autograph of a very formal star!

Although these up turns in Brian and Jean's fortunes were welcome it was another far more lucrative piece of Sweet merchandise that paved the way for Brian's son and heir to be born.

1991

# Def, A Leopard From Heaven

**Surprises** come in many shapes and sizes and a lucky envelope can land on the doormat at any time. For ordinary folk a windfall will likely be the result of a lottery win or inheritance. For pop folk, especially aged pop folk who were once stars, stars who wrote some hits, a windfall comes in the form of a cover version.

In October 1993 Def Leopard's management sought permission for the band to record a version of Sweet's song 'Action'. They wanted not only to record it but also to use it as a single. This was the clincher, the factor that would turn it all around for Andy, Steve, Mick and especially Brian. Permission was duly granted with a proviso that half the royalties be paid in advance. They had been screwed before, that was after all what the song 'Action' was written about.

With his 'Action' money and his income from BCs Sweet Brian had enough to buy a farm not far from Maple Cross. This was what he longed for but to please his partner Jean he ditched the farm idea in place of a large house in Denham, again just a mile or so from Maple Cross and only a little further from his one time home town of Harefield.

At last at the age of forty-eight he had clawed his way back from total oblivion to a life of luxury. He had a mortgage on his home but there were further royalties to come from 'Action', bookings were up with his band and he had a new partner. As always the only cloud on the horizon was the status of his health. His kidneys did not always function well and his tremors were always present. Brian was certainly never an intellectual at any time in his life, he was very much a bread and butter man mentally, however there was a point in the late eighties when he seemed easily confused, when his statements in interviews didn't always make perfect sense.

The worst time for this seems to be around the making of the Sweet's 'Ballroom Blitz' Video. Happily this was not a decline that continued and Brian's mind had become sharper by the mid 90s. One thing guaranteed to cloud his mind was tiredness and he learned to rest and pace himself as the 90s rolled by. Brian wrote a song that begged the question "how much longer will this fight go on" just months before he died.

The album Lets Go contains some remarkable performances from Brian Connolly. He was now a semi invalid, having trouble walking and in poor systemic health. His head and arms shook relentlessly and his skin was blotchy, an outward sign of poor liver and kidney function.
He had not drunk alcohol in over a decade or taken drugs in years but his decline continued unabated.

# Lets go!!!!!!!!!!!

**Reinvigorated** by the Birth of Brian junior and the money from 'Action' Brian assembled some musicians and wrote three new songs, these were part of a batch of more re recordings of The Sweet's back catalogue, all found their way onto the album Let's Go.

The production on the record is dubious and claims to be a re creation of what one would hear at a BC Sweet concert. It would have been better if some audience noise and applause had been dubbed onto the album, thus really re creating the atmosphere of a live LP. As released, the album's concept does not really work and it is possible that the "recreation of live" claim was a late addition to the sleeve notes in an attempt to excuse the poor production.

The new songs are amazingly good, lyrically they are all autobiographical in some way, and musically they have obviously been written to assuage the deficiencies in his vocals. The production is so totally "spit and sawdust" that the deficiencies are still painfully obvious but the three new songs are "art". They contain power and emotion that most believed was long gone from his grasp, they are poignant in a way that sort of evokes a fatally wounded phoenix rising from the ashes just one more time to take its final triumphant bow.

"Wait till morning comes" is a wonderful song co written by Brian that gave a clue that Brian knew his chances of seeing his son grow up were slim. The lines

"I'm not looking for excuses anymore" and "how much longer must this fight go on" are very poignant and telling. Like wise his song Lets Go is a wonderful biographical journey, Brian telling us that "I've been in every town and sung on every stage but still the crowd comes in to join the show" The chorus of the song is entirely borrowed from Chinn and Chapman's intro for 'Ballroom Blitz', probably till the very day he died Brian Connolly was capable of screaming Lets go in a totally inimitable way, there will never be another like him in this respect. The song Do it again is a passable composition reminiscent of Status quo in their heyday.

The album is let down by its production which seems to be because of two factors, one would have been money the other skill. It is without doubt that this independently financed LP would have been made on a tiny budget but clever use of studio electronics and production techniques could have saved the day. At fifty Brian was way behind the times with regard just how much could be done behind the mixing desks of the mid 90s.

The album does not actually give credit to anyone as producer. The musicians playing on the songs are Glen Williams, Guitar. David Glover, Base. Dave Farmer, Drums with Steve Mulvey on Keyboards. These were the men who played for Brian in the 1990s and right up until he died. Immediately after Brian's passing his canny backing musicians re released the album Let's go under the title The Definitive Brian Connolly's Sweet. They added two numbers to the set, a cover of 'Love Is Like Oxygen' and a cover of Magic Circle. Both of these additions are far better produced than the bulk of the album but of course do not contain Brian's vocals. The master stroke for selling the album was without doubt the addition of 'The Magic Circle', for many years this excellent track had remained unreleased, an 80s memory cherished by those at Brian's early solo concerts. The album sold almost entirely by the promise that it contained Brian's 1985 version of the song sadly it did not.

Some years after Brian's passing a group of Mega mixers re mixed and used electronic pitch adjustment on Brian's "hits" from Let's Go. The resultant album Brian Connolly's Sweet… The greatest Hits re mixed, is remarkable. It truly shows that with the aid of modern technology Brian could have recorded vocals that once "adjusted" would have sounded professional and acceptable to quite a wide audience. Plans are afoot to re master many of his post sweet recordings, adding instrumentation where necessary or in the case of later material building new music tracks around his re mixed and treated vocals. These techniques have become common in the years since Brian passed away and have helped many who can barely sing to achieve considerable success. Brian was a man who for many years certainly could sing and who left the world some sterling vocal performances. Surely a far more fitting use of these technical advances is to enhance his legacy where his endeavours were spoiled due to ill health.
Lets Go in its present form is interesting but not joyous, this is a quality problem. Let's hope that Brian's restoration in sound is swift and his fans soon have re recorded versions of his solo legacy.

By a very strange coincidence Brian Connolly's last recorded performance in a studio was with Frank Torpey. In July 1996 Brian popped by to visit his old friend in Harrow. They had talked about recording something for a while however Torpey recalls that Brian's time and "appointment keeping" habits were in another dimension.

On the day in question Brian was several hours late, probably due to performance nerves. The song in question was a Torpey composition called "Sharontina". Many years before Brian had demoed a song called Elivita and the two are vaguely similar in parts though this is certainly a coincidence. Sharontina is a rock song with a slight grunge feel. It is not a great melody and exists only in a demo form, though very well recorded. Brian was by now in terrible health and his ability to perform was greatly impaired yet Torpey managed to record a pretty steady performance. One reason for this is because the song has no real range requirements for Brian as a singer

This leaves the song a little flat and one day Frank hopes to add harmonies in order to flesh out the song. "Her name was Sharontina she came from Argentina, Buenos Aires we love you" was a lyrical turn of phrase destined for oblivion until it became the final recording by the man who sang 'Blockbuster'. Because of his early contribution to Sweet and his continued friendship with Mick and Brian, Torpey was invited to Brian's memorial show at the London Camden palace. He pressed two thousand copies of Sharontina and other numbers on an Album entitled "Sweeter" and to his credit sold the lot. It is quite a claim to fame to have been on Brian's first record but to have written and played on his last one thirty years later is truly remarkable.

# Stabbed In The Back

In 1996 Brian took part in a documentary for channel four, the resultant product was a travesty. The program was produced by Gwyneth Lloyd and directed by James Marsh. From the start it is obvious that the program's aim was purely to portray Brian as a pathetic figure. This ploy needed careful editing and camera work to be achieved but the results were catastrophic. Camera credits go to Mike Coles, Colin Chase and James Haliday. Together they filmed Brian from beneath the dash of his car, struggling to walk around Butlins, doubled over in pain and in a thousand unflattering vignettes, deliberately lit to enhance Brian's wrinkles and shakes. The music is dark and evocative of a horror movie.

The title of the program is 'Don't Leave Me This Way'. Brian 's first appearance on screen is in close up, a close up so severe that no one would look half decent but the effect on a fifty-year-old man whose head shook un controllably was devastating. The program makers knew exactly what they were doing. Brian speaks perfect sense but a lot of what he says would have been lost on the evening of transmission because of the shock factor.

Next we see a billboard showing that Sweet are appearing at Butlins Holiday Park for five weeks throughout the summer. Also appearing were; Marty Wilde, Showaddywaddy, Bucks Fizz and Edwin

Star. Butlins and Pontins are used as metaphors for the old expression "at the end of the pier" Their theatres and dance halls are the natural home of entertainers from fifteen or twenty years before. Mummy and Daddy can leave the young ones with a Camp babysitter and enjoy a trip back to their youth while on holiday. It is almost an exact science when booking acts for these holiday parks. The sixties are now too long ago for the acts of that time to appeal to young parents, the eighties kids are just about to come on line but in 1996 when this dreadful program was made the 70s was the perfect era to offer up as holiday entertainment. Next we see Brian and his family outside his large Denham house, once again in a sunlit exaggerated close up Brian gives perfect directions to his band for the address of a venue. No one would look good filmed in this manner but things get worse when the program cuts to the interior of his car and another unflattering shot, face only.

Ex wife Marilyn then talks about his early life, she is filmed in a typical head and shoulders well lit interview shot and looks bright and attractive. Of all the participants and interviewees only Marilyn manages to escape the editors clutches, she does not bad mouth her ailing ex husband and the program makers have to be content with her fond memories and sympathetic opinions regarding the father of her children. Her conscience should be clear, for although it had been very unwise to partake in such a disgusting betrayal, she obviously went into the project with no idea how cruel it would be.

Next the band describe their early years and day jobs, all are filmed in the normal way, in a studio, with a backdrop and flattering lighting.

Everything about being on Television is artificial, there is virtually no natural way to light a scene as the camera does not make the adjustments that a human eyes does, so program makers must choose how a scene is lit and how flattering it is for its subjects.

Nicky Chinn talks, looking great, in a studio setting, perfectly well lit. Brian Connolly re appears filmed from beneath the dash of his car, his hand looks enormous as he hold his chin, both are trembling violently before the camera perched just inches below. As if this wasn't enough the producer now adds the ghastly horror music. Clips and cuts show Brian and Steve in their heyday while Marilyn talks about his make up wearing days. Then an insight is offered. Like all "stars" Brian was detached and totally focussed on becoming a star. There follows a poignant few moments where the music is sentimental and the band describe the loneliness of life on the road.

At no time has Brian been portrayed in a flattering or even sympathetic light. All inter cut scenes that lead to Brian are edited for dramatic effect showing youth and then dilapidation. The horror music is only ever used when Brian is on screen.

Toward the end of the program Brian is seen travelling to the theatre where he is about to perform, the camera is trained obsessively on his trembling hand for nine seconds, that is all that is on screen, Brian's trembling hand. This disgusting and shameful exploitation of a partially disabled person would probably not be allowed today.

Hearts were breaking across the country the night Channel four screened this repulsive travesty of television journalism. Brian arrives at the venue and there is a bunch of "yobs" outside who mock him "sort your strides out mate" and "who are you" were shouted from faceless bystanders as Brian limps into the venue. Why was this shown? What purpose could the drunken insults of heartless youths have served other than to rub it on one more time that Brian Connolly was a semi invalid who walked with difficulty?

Andy and Brian are set against each other in clips, Andy filmed in a studio with good lighting, Brian in a corridor, in a close up so tight that his fringe is not even visible the lighting is appalling. It is not clear just how much Andy wanted to destroy Brian but his comments and the "cross edit" direct shots of Brian were devastating on the night of broadcast. Andy describes how one cannot unfry an egg; one has to see how it turns out. The next shot is of a poorly lit Brian Connolly. Immediately Steve Priest puts his hands in the air and exclaims that he can't unscramble an egg and low and behold Brian is all over the screen again. This evil manipulation of image and sound has persisted for more than twenty minutes and it is amongst the most shameful ever inflicted on an individual via the medium of television.

There are a few clips of Brian performing with his band but again he is not allowed to shine, no one from the cameraman to the producer bothered to properly film so much as twenty seconds of him entertaining the crowd obviously there to see him. If it was filmed, it certainly was not in the program.

Finally Marilyn begs the question "was it all worth it" and answers it herself; she believes he would say it had all been worth it.

The one clever and exciting moment in the program is the eerie and urgent way his ascent to the stage is presented, with horror like sound effects and a raft of TV screens showing the band when they were young, the screens slightly distorted to add to the whole edgy feel. Had Brian then been given a moment to shine, filmed from a distance at a point in the show when the audience were singing and clapping, which they were, Brian could have at least had a moment of glory. Sadly no, a repeat shot of him during rehearsal was inserted, making it look like he had been helped onto the stage during a performance. None of his determination or bravery is ever portrayed on camera or in the commentary.

The most wicked piece of Television broadcast in the UK in 1996 ends with Brian backstage talking to just one fan, informing the man that he was once a bit famous but is a has been now. Just one fan is all the program makers could bare to allow on this glam rock blood letting. Brian Connolly still has many fans, possibly many thousands and it is now over a decade since his death. It would have taken little effort to have informed and assembled a dozen or so fans needed when a star such as he was on parade. In 1997 there were plenty of fans who would have shown themselves had they known about the program or been contacted through fan clubs. To end Brian is filmed walking with his now "so familiar" limp off toward a wilderness of holiday chalets, as he slips into the darkness he sings a chorus of the soul song 'Don't Leave Me This Way'. The screen goes blank and the list of shame begins, the dire editing, always cutting to Brian looking awful was the work of Colin Knijff; the producer was Gwyneth Lloyd and the director James Marsh.

There is a postscript informing us of the whereabouts of the band members, we are reminded that Steve lives in California, Mick has retired and Andy still tours with his Sweet. We are not told that they will all deeply regret their involvement in this misrepresentation and exploitation of a sick man. At his funeral they will have uncomfortable moments of silence to consider their dreadful mistake, not just in participating but in the contributions they provided channel four's program makers.

The postscript obviously does not say that on the night the "show" was broadcast, watched by millions, its subject was truly heartbroken and that he never fully recovered from being so wickedly humiliated.

The final scene in the documentary where Brian is seated talking to his "fan" does have one redeeming feature. Brian is smiling and joking with the fan and seems very at ease with his status as a "has been". The term "has been" came into use in the 1930s and was first widely used to describe Hollywood's former silent movie stars.

It soon became a derogative term for all in show business whose careers had long passed peak. It is never kind to describe some one as a "has been" and Brian was wise indeed to take power over the phrase and re claim it for himself. For those who enter the realm of pop stardom the realm of "has been dom" will follow within a few years. The documentary about Brian begins with a ridiculous statement that "Singer Brian Connolly is attempting a comeback" this hackneyed, clichéd; Sunday paper expression really exposes the crassness of the entire project. Totally unprepared to "lie" and provide Brian with a few fans at the end of the program or light him in a way that minimised his age or tremors, the makers were however prepared to make a totally false statement. *Singer Brian Connolly* had been working non-stop in the UK for fifteen years since he had left Sweet.

This was simply a sensationalised account of his life and his health problems and took little steps to display or describe his dogged determination to continue to perform when most others would have been in a wheel chair.

# February 9th, 1997

**Shattered** by the broadcast of the channel four documentary and by the recent break up of his relationship with Jean, Brian found himself alone in a mansion house in Denham. Sadly after all the years he had spent clawing his way back to a life of luxury, he would not live long enough to enjoy the spoils of his long war against his disease. After his death the large house was sold to football star Neil Shipperley.

Brian's confidence had all but deserted him, though in any case he was now too ill to perform. Jean had moved out around the time of the broadcast taking Brian junior with her. Obviously it cannot have been easy for the young mum coping with the pressures of looking after a young baby and a very sick partner too.

Brian's final concert was in Bristol on December 5th 1996. By New Year of 1997 Brian's health was a concern to all who knew him. His band had continued to honour bookings but he had been unable to join them. This would later become a bone of contention as they "continued to continue" to honour bookings in the months and subsequently years after his death. One cannot blame them really as they had played 'Blockbuster' more times than anyone except Andy Scott himself. Brian had actually dispensed with their services shortly before he died after discovering that they were continuing to honour his bookings, with out his knowledge. To this very day BC s Sweet are performing what has become a tribute show somewhere in a town near you!

At the end of January Brian was admitted to hospital, his Kidney problems were now critical and the doctors held out little hope for his recovery. This scenario had played out several times in his life so there was wide spread disbelief at the prognosis, Brian had survived all these years on borrowed time, surely he would have the last laugh one more time.

He discharged himself after several days, deciding that he would like to die at home, both Nicola and Michele his daughters had been looking after him since his relationship with Jean had ended though she was far from estranged from him at this point.

After three days at home Brian was re admitted to hospital with Kidney failure. Friends were called to pay their last respects and he was never short of company or comfort at the hospital. As the end came nearer Andy Scott paid a visit to Brian's bedside and as is often the case when the end is near, the years of bitterness and dispute seemed to roll away. By all accounts Andy spent quite a while with Brian and it is said that they hatched a plan. If Brian made it through then they could tour together, not as one band but in a similar way to when Brian had toured with MUD. Andy and his band would perform a set of the heavier Sweet numbers and then Brian would come on to do a smaller set of the hits. This would have been a great compromise at any time during the previous decade but they were out of time.

By 8pm on Sunday 9th February 1997 Brian was slipping away, his family were there gathered around his bed as his struggle with years of appalling ill health finally came to a close. It was decided that to obey his wishes and send him home again would be futile, he was simply too weak to have survived the short journey.

He died at 9.45 pm from multiple organ failure.

For one week Brian Connolly's image and name were world news, he made the front pages of countless papers, some taking the time to write balanced articles about his life, triumphs, trials and tribulations and dogged determination not to give in. Others went for the same re hashed clichéd stories, giving the public a rather distorted view of his circumstances toward the end of his life. On TV his death was deemed very note worthy and all the major channels reported live from his funeral in Denham. Queen's Brian May paid a written tribute, saying that Brian would be greatly missed, had a wonderful voice and that Sweet's records were amongst the best of their time. Nicky Chinn read a moving tribute and despite some cold February weather more than three hundred fans were present along with the worlds media, all assembled to say a saddened farewell to the man who sang 'Blockbuster'.

To have Brian Connolly for a father must have been a unique experience for Nicola and Michele Connolly. It cannot have been easy from the simple point of his estrangement and divorce from their mother Marilyn. Then there were the years of touring in the late seventies when he was away for long periods of their childhood. By the time they were at school their father's life in the fast lane was over and with it went their luxurious lifestyle. As teenagers they would have no doubt felt a little embarrassed by their father's very public health and financial problems. All teenagers feel too cool to be seen in public with their square old parents without the added burden of them being yesterdays rock stars. Brian junior will have no memories of the father who left him when he was only a baby.

Hopefully all three of his children can take comfort in the musical legacy their father recorded during the 1970s and the fact that he is still remembered with great affection almost fifty years after he began his career and more than a decade after his passing. The voice of the family now seems to be daughter Nicola who always speaks of her father with much fondness and pride. Who knows perhaps one day in the not too distant future Brian Connolly junior may take to the stage with a band or even Steve Priest, now that would be amazing.

Brian Connolly was a 'Hell Raiser' for sure in his youth but most of his excesses were simply an attempt to cover his feelings of insecurity. His demise was entirely caused by his own actions and a fluke of nature that meant that while most of his peers enjoyed similar indulgences, they recovered. We all choose to believe that it won't be "us" each time we smoke a cigarette or eat a burger, or perhaps we have some stronger vices, what ever they are, to enjoy them we must believe that we are not going to be the one who is harmed by them. Brian was in some ways destined to live a short life, not as short as Marc Bolan perhaps but time was always a luxury for Brian Connolly.

There have been far bigger stars, better singers too but who would have known back in Hamilton just what a remarkable impact the young tot given up for adoption would make on the world.

The fans of fatally flawed stars, stars whose demise is apparent in their work are fans that forgive and accommodate. Those who demand perfection in a life and career will not be satisfied by the likes of Brian Connolly. In many ways he was just a man who sang some songs, beautifully when younger, with a voice so distinctive that it is impossible to emulate fully. He remains irreplaceable to this very day, never more so than when Andy Scott and his musicians perform what are very accomplished and well attended shows. Brian is always there, within the hearts of those in the audience, they will always carry Brian Connolly back to the Sweet and will sing for him with their own voices.

# NICKY CHINN & MIKE CHAPMAN

## The UK HIT Singles

'Funny Funny' The Sweet January 1971 No 13 Silver

'Tom Tom Turnaround' New World May 1971 No 6 Silver

'Co Co' The Sweet June 1971 No 2 Gold

'Alexander Graham Bell' The Sweet Oct 1971 No 33

Kara Kara New World Dec 1971 No 19

'Poppa Joe' The Sweet Feb 1972 No 11 Silver

Sister Jane New World Apr 1972 No 9 Silver

'Little Willy' The Sweet June 1972 No 4 Gold

'Wig Wam Bam' The Sweet Nov 1972 No 4 Gold

'Blockbuster' The Sweet Jan 1973 No 1 Gold

Roof top singing New World Feb 1973 No 50

'Crazy' MUD Mar 1973 No 12

'Hell Raiser' The Sweet Apr 1973 No 2 Silver

Can The Can S. Quattro May 1973 No 1 Gold

Hypnosis MUD June 1973 No 17

48 Crash S. Quattro July 1973 No 3 Silver

The 'Ballroom Blitz' The Sweet Sept 1973 No 2 Gold

Daytona Demon S Quattro Oct 1973 No 14

Dyne Mite MUD Dec 1973 No 4 Silver

'Tiger Feet' MUD Jan 1974 No 1 Gold

'Teenage Rampage' SWEET Jan 1974 No 2 Gold

Devil Gate Drive S. Quattro Feb 1974 No 1 Gold

The Cat Crept in MUD April 1974 No 2 Gold

Touch Too Much   The Arrows   May 1974 No 8 Silver

Too Big S. Quattro June 1974 No 14

Rocket MUD July 1974 No 6 Silver

'The Sixteens' SWEET Aug 1974 No 9 Gold

'Turn It Down' SWEET Nov 1974 No 41

The Wild One S. Quattro Nov 1974 No 7 Silver

Lonely This Christmas MUD Dec 1974 No 1 Gold

Last Night With You The Arrows Feb 1975 No 25

Secrets That you Keep MUD Mar 1975 No 3 Silver

Mama Wont Like Me S. Quattro Apr 1975 No 31

If you think you know how to love me June 1975 No 3 silver ( Smokie)

Moonshine Sally MUD July 1975 No 10 silver

Don't play your rock n roll to me Oct 1975 No 8 Silver (Smokie)

Somthings been making me blue Jan 1976 No 17

Ill meet you at Midnight Smokie Sep 1976 No 11 silver

Living Next Door to Alice Smokie Nov 1976 No 5 Gold

Tear Me Apart S. Quattro Mar 1977 No 27

Lay Back in the arms of someone Smokie Apr 1977 No 12 Silver

Its your Life Smokie Jul 1977 No 5 Silver

For A Few Dollars More Smokie Jan 1978 No 17

If you Cant give me love S.Quattro Mar 1978 No 4 silver

Oh Carol Smokie May 1978 No 5 Gold

The Race is on S. Quattro Jul 1978 No 43

Lay your love on me RACEY Oct 1978 No 3 Gold

Mexican Girl SMOKIE Nov 1978 No 19

Stumblin in S.Quattro/C Norman Nov 1978 No 41

Some Girls RACEY Mar 1979 No 2 Gold

Boy Oh Boy RACEY Aug 1979 No 22

She's in love with you S. Quattro Oct 1979 No 11
Never Been in love S. Quattro May 1980 No 56

Mickey Toni Basil Jan 1982 No 2 Gold

## SWEET

### UK Hit Singles

| | |
|---|---|
| January 1971 'Funny Funny' | 13 Silver |
| June 1971 'CO CO' | 2 Gold |
| October 1971 'Alexander Graham Bell' | 33 |
| February 1972 'Poppa Joe' | 11 Silver |
| June 1972 'Little Willy' | 4 Gold |
| Nove 1972 'Wig Wam Bam' | 4 Gold |
| January 1973 'Blockbuster' | 1 Gold |
| April 1973 'Hell Raiser' | 2 Silver |
| Sept 1973 The 'Ballroom Blitz' | 2 Gold |
| January 1974 'Teenage Rampage' | 2 Gold |
| July 1974 'The Sixteens' | 9 Gold |
| Dec 1974 'Turn It Down' | 41 |
| February 1975 'Fox On The Run' * | 2 Silver |
| August 1975 'Action' * | 15 |
| January 1976 'Lies In Your Eyes' * | 35 |
| January 1978 'Love Is Like Oxygen' # | 9 Silver |
| January 1985 Its It's the Sweet Mix | 45 |

All titles written by Nicky Chinn and Mike Chapman except:


\* By Connolly, Scott, Tucker, Priest
# By Scott/ Griffin


Sweet Mix contains the following titles:

'Blockbuster', The 'Ballroom Blitz', 'Fox On The Run', 'Hell Raiser'.

## SWEET'S GERMAN HIT SINGLES

1971 to 1979

| | |
|---|---|
| April 1971 'Funny Funny' ** | 5 |
| July 1971 'Co Co' ** | 1 |
| Oct 1971 'Alexander Graham Bell' ** | 24 |
| Mar 1972 'Poppa Joe' ** | 3 |
| Jun 1972 'Little Willy' ** | 1 |
| Nove 1972 'Wig Wam Bam' ** | 1 |
| Feb 1973 'Blockbuster' ** | 1 |
| May 1973 'Hell Raiser' ** | 1 |
| Sept 1973 The 'Ballroom Blitz' ** | 1 |
| Jan 1974 'Teenage Rampage' ** | 1 |
| June 1974 'The Sixteens' ** | 4 |
| Dec 1974 'Turn It Down' ** | 4 |
| Mar 1975 'Fox On The Run' * | 1 |
| July 1975 'Action'* | 2 |
| Jan 1976 'Lies In Your Eyes'* | 5 |
| Jul 1976 'Lost Angels' * | 13 |
| Mar 1977 'Fever Of Love' * | 9 |

Aug 1977 'Stairway To The Stars' *       15

Feb 1978 'Love Is Like Oxygen' #         10

Aug 1978 California Nights +             23

Mar 1979 'Call Me' ~                     29


Written By:
~   A Scott
+   Scott Tucker Priest Connolly
#   Scott / Griffin
*   Connolly Scott Tucker Priest
**  Chinn / Chapman

## SWEET V QUEEN

On The German Front !

Below is a comparative list of all Sweet's and Queen's hits in Germany. It is worth noting that Sweet's hits appear in true order of release while Queen's hits were sporadic coming months and occasionally years apart.

| | |
|---|---|
| 'Funny Funny' | 5 |
| Killer Queen | 12 |
| 'Co Co' | 1 |
| Bohemian Rhapsody | 7 |
| 'Alexander Graham Bell' | 24 |
| We are the champions | 13 |
| 'Poppa Joe' | 3 |
| Fat Bottom Girls | 27 |
| 'Little Willy' | 1 |
| Don't Stop Me Now | 35 |
| 'Wig Wam Bam' | 1 |
| 'Crazy' Little Thing Called Love | 13 |
| 'Blockbuster' | 1 |
| Save Me | 40 |
| 'Hell Raiser' | 1 |
| Another One Bites The Dust | 7 |
| The 'Ballroom Blitz' | 1 |
| Flash | 3 |
| 'Teenage Rampage' | 1 |
| Under Pressure | 27 |
| 'The Sixteens' | 4 |
| Body Language | 27 |
| 'Turn It Down' | 4 |
| Radio Ga Ga | 2 |
| 'Fox On The Run' | 1 |
| I Want To Break Free | 5 |

| | |
|---|---|
| 'Action' | 2 |
| It's a Kinda Magic | 6 |
| 'Lies In Your Eyes' | 5 |
| I want it all | 11 |
| 'Lost Angels' | 13 |
| Inuendo | 5 |
| Fever O f Love | 9 |
| Show Must Go On | 7 |
| 'Stairway To The Stars' | 15 |
| Heaven for everyone | 15 |
| 'Love Is Like Oxygen' | 10 |
| No comparable Queen single | // |
| California Nights | 23 |
| No Comparable Queen single | // |
| 'Call Me' | 29 |

As this list amply demonstrates Queen never enjoyed even a half of the phenomenal success achieved by Sweet either with or without Chinn and Chapman. In Germany Sweet wore the crown, not Queen.

Brian Connolly's entire solo recording out put
1979-1996

Sept 1979 'Don't You Know A Lady' Single Polydor

Sept 1979 Phone you (b side) Polydor

Apr 1980 Take away the music Single Polydor

Apr 1980 Alabama Man (b side) Polydor


1980 LADY Un released Demo version
1980 Sunshine days Unreleased Demo Version


Feb 1982 Hypnotised Single (Carriere) RCA
Feb 1982 Fade Away (b side) RCA

1983 Old Folks Un Released Demo version


Songs for the proposed album JAILBAIT
(1984)

| 'THE MAGIC CIRCLE' | released Malibu records 2002 |
| --- | --- |
| Jailbait | Unfinished master recording |
| Red Haired Rage | Early demo version |
| The final show | Demo Version |

Oct 1987 'Poppa Joe' The Unitone Rockers ft Brian Connolly
 (Released Malibu Records…)

July 1989 Re recordings:

'Wig Wam Bam' 'Little Willy' and 'Blockbuster'
(Released as "Hits of the 70s" ( Long island Records ltd )
Oct 1995 Album Lets Go ( BAM Records)

Re recordings:
'Action', 'Ballroom Blitz', 'Hell Raiser', 'Little Willy', 'Blockbuster', 'Wig Wam Bam', 'Fox On The Run', Burn on the flame,
'Teenage Rampage'

New Material on album:

| Wait 'til Morning comes | (Connolly/Williams) |
| Lets' go | (Connolly/Earle) |
| Do it again | (Connolly/Earle) |

May 1996   Sharontina   (Torpey)   Demo version

(this is the last known studio recording of Brian Connolly)